THE NEAR ASSASSINATION OF DONALD TRUMP

Story of How and Why He Won the 2024 America Election

Daniel K. Fleenor

ISBN: 978-1-257-95859-7

Published by: Sharp Press

INTRODUCTION

The sun was beginning its descent over the rolling hills of Butler County, Pennsylvania, casting long shadows across the Butler Farm Show Grounds as thousands of red-hatted supporters streamed toward the outdoor stage. It was 6:03 PM on July 13, 2024, and Donald Trump was eight minutes into what would become the most consequential campaign rally in American political history. The former president, dressed in his signature navy suit and red tie, stood behind a modest podium, gesticulating enthusiastically as he delivered familiar refrains about border security and economic prosperity to an energized crowd of approximately 8,000 people. Behind him, a massive American flag fluttered in the warm evening breeze, creating the perfect backdrop for what appeared to be just another stop on the campaign trail toward his attempted return to the White House.

In that moment, with Trump pointing toward a chart displaying immigration statistics, none of the 8,000 people gathered in that Pennsylvania field could have imagined they were about to witness an event that would fundamentally alter the trajectory of American politics. Not the Secret Service agents scanning the crowd. Not the local law enforcement positioned around the perimeter. Not the media representatives documenting what they assumed would be standard campaign fare. And certainly not the 78-year-old former president himself, who was about to experience something that would transform him from a controversial political figure into what his supporters would call a divinely protected survivor, and what historians would later recognize as the catalyst for one of the most remarkable political comebacks in American history.

The Moment That Defined a Presidency

At exactly 6:11 PM, as Trump turned slightly to his right to reference the immigration chart behind him, the sharp crack of gunfire shattered the summer evening air. Eight shots rang out in rapid succession from an AR-15-style rifle, fired by 20-year-old Thomas Matthew Crooks from the roof of a building approximately 130 yards away. In those terrifying seconds, as chaos erupted and Secret Service agents rushed the stage, a single bullet grazed Trump's right ear, missing his head by mere millimeters. One rally attendee, 50-year-old volunteer firefighter Corey Comperatore, was killed instantly while shielding his family. Two others were critically wounded. The would-be assassin was neutralized by a Secret Service sniper just twelve seconds after opening fire.

But it wasn't the assassination attempt itself that would reshape the 2024 election—it was what happened next. As Secret Service agents swarmed around the wounded former president, urging him to evacuate immediately, Trump did something that defied both protocol and human instinct. Rising from behind the podium where he had taken cover, blood streaming down the right side of his face, Trump thrust his fist into the air and shouted three words that would echo through the remainder of the campaign: "Fight! Fight! Fight!" The image captured by Associated Press photographer Evan Vucci—a bloodied but defiant Trump, fist raised against the backdrop of the American flag, surrounded by Secret Service agents—would become one of the most powerful political photographs in modern American history.

From Victim to Victor

This book tells the extraordinary story of how those eight seconds of gunfire on a summer evening in Pennsylvania became the turning point that propelled Donald Trump back to the presidency. It is the story of how a near-death experience transformed not just a candidate, but an entire movement. How the bullet that grazed Trump's ear on July 13th became, in the minds of millions of Americans, evidence of divine intervention in the democratic process. How the image of his bloodied but unbowed figure pumping his fist became a symbol of resilience that resonated far beyond his traditional base of supporters.

The connection between survival and electoral success is not immediately obvious, nor was it guaranteed. In the hours following the shooting, political analysts across the spectrum debated whether the assassination attempt would help or hurt Trump's chances. Some predicted a sympathy vote that would boost his polling numbers. Others worried that the violence would remind voters of the chaos that seemed to follow Trump throughout his political career. Few could have predicted that the event would become the foundation of a narrative so powerful it would carry Trump not just to victory, but to one of the most decisive electoral wins in recent American history.

The Narrative That Won the White House

What happened in Butler, Pennsylvania, was more than an assassination attempt—it was the birth of a political legend. In the weeks and months that followed, Trump and his campaign masterfully wove the events of July 13th into a larger story about providence, perseverance, and the idea that he was destined to save America. The bandaged ear that Trump wore to the Republican

National Convention just three days later became a symbol of his sacrifice. The "Fight! Fight! Fight!" chant became a rallying cry at every subsequent campaign event. The narrative of divine protection became central to his appeal among religious voters who saw his survival as evidence that God wanted him to be president.

This story is told through exclusive interviews with campaign officials, Secret Service agents, rally attendees, and political analysts who witnessed these events unfold. It draws upon thousands of pages of congressional testimony, FBI investigative reports, and previously unreported details about both the assassination attempt and the campaign's strategic response. Most importantly, it examines how a single moment of violence and Trump's instinctive reaction to it created a powerful emotional connection with voters that transcended traditional political loyalties and ultimately delivered him the presidency.

Why This Story Matters

The 2024 election will be remembered for many reasons: the first time a former president won a non-consecutive second term since Grover Cleveland, the decisive victory that included winning the popular vote, and the realignment of various voter demographics. But above all, it will be remembered as the election where a bullet changed everything. Where eight seconds of chaos became four years of power. Where the difference between death and political resurrection was measured in millimeters.

Understanding how Trump's near-assassination became his path back to the presidency is crucial for understanding not just the 2024 election, but the current state of American democracy itself. It reveals how quickly political narratives can be reshaped by dramatic events, how voters respond to displays of physical courage under fire, and how the line between victimhood and leadership can become blurred in the modern media landscape. This is the story of how Donald Trump turned the worst moment of his campaign into his greatest asset, and how the American people responded by giving him another chance to lead their nation.

The events of July 13, 2024, lasted just eight seconds. Their political consequences will shape American politics for generations to come.

CHAPTER 1: A NATION DIVIDED

America in early 2024 felt like a country teetering on the edge of something unprecedented. The familiar rhythms of democratic governance had been replaced by a constant state of political warfare, where every policy disagreement became an existential battle and every election carried the weight of national survival. Social media algorithms amplified the most extreme voices while drowning out moderate perspectives, creating echo chambers that reinforced the belief that political opponents weren't just wrong—they were dangerous enemies of the republic itself. Trust in institutions had eroded to historic lows, with polls showing that nearly half of Americans believed their democracy was in serious jeopardy.

Into this volatile atmosphere stepped Donald Trump, seeking an unprecedented return to power after his 2020 defeat and the chaos of January 6th. His candidacy represented more than a typical political comeback; it was a test of whether American democracy could contain the forces it had unleashed. The stage was set for a campaign unlike any in modern history, where the stakes felt genuinely existential and the potential for violence lurked beneath every rally, every debate, and every election night. Few could have predicted that this dangerous political climate would soon be punctuated by actual gunfire, transforming an already explosive election into something far more dramatic and consequential.

The Political Climate of 2024

The United States entered 2024 as a nation fundamentally at odds with itself, divided not just by policy preferences but by entirely different versions of reality. Some four in every five voters felt the

U.S. was "spiraling" out of control, with 86% agreeing that "acts of violence" were "throwing this country into chaos" during a turbulent election year. The traditional shared foundation of American civic life—agreement on basic facts, respect for democratic institutions, and acceptance of electoral outcomes—had crumbled under the weight of partisan polarization and deliberate disinformation campaigns.

Social media platforms had become battlegrounds where competing narratives about everything from election integrity to public health measures created parallel universes of information. Mainstream media outlets were viewed with deep suspicion by large segments of the population, while alternative news sources and conspiracy theories filled the vacuum left by declining trust in traditional journalism. This information chaos created a political environment where compromise became nearly impossible, as different factions couldn't even agree on what problems needed solving.

The economic anxieties that had been building since the 2008 financial crisis, compounded by the COVID-19 pandemic's disruptions and subsequent inflation, provided fertile ground for populist appeals on both sides of the political spectrum. Americans increasingly viewed politics through a zero-sum lens, where their side's victory required not just defeating opponents but completely discrediting them. This winner-take-all mentality transformed routine political competition into something resembling tribal warfare, with devastating consequences for democratic norms and civil discourse.

Rising Tensions and Partisan Violence

Political violence, once considered an aberration in American democracy, had become a regular feature of the political landscape by 2024. Since the 2020 election and continuing into the 2024 election, the election denial movement prompted thousands of death threats directed at election workers, officials, and their families, with some receiving letters laced with fentanyl. The January 6th Capitol attack had shattered the taboo against political violence, creating a new normal where threats against public officials were routine and extreme rhetoric regularly crossed into calls for armed resistance.

Additional polling found that 42% of Americans thought it was likely there would be a civil war within the next 10 years, including 14% who thought this was very likely. This wasn't merely academic speculation—it reflected a genuine belief among significant portions of the population that democratic institutions had failed and that violence might be necessary to protect their vision of America. Political rallies increasingly required heavy security, while elected officials faced credible threats that forced them to alter their daily routines and public appearances.

The normalization of violent rhetoric created an atmosphere where extreme language became commonplace, with politicians and media figures regularly describing their opponents in existential terms. Social media platforms struggled to contain content that danced on the line between protected speech and incitement to violence. The cumulative effect was a political culture where the unthinkable had become thinkable, where discussions of political violence were no longer relegated to the fringes but had entered mainstream political discourse. This escalating climate of hostility would prove to be the perfect storm that made the events of July 13th not just possible, but perhaps inevitable.

Trump's Return to the Political Stage

Donald Trump's decision to seek the presidency again represented one of the most audacious political comebacks in American history. Four years after leaving Washington as a pariah, following his attempt to overturn the 2020 election to stay in office, Trump's victory defied two assassination attempts, two presidential impeachments, his criminal conviction, and many other criminal charges. His return to politics was motivated by a toxic combination of personal grievance, genuine belief that the 2020 election had been stolen, and an unshakeable conviction that only he could save America from what he saw as radical left-wing destruction.

The former president's path back to political relevance was paved with legal challenges that, paradoxically, only strengthened his hold on the Republican base. Each indictment and court appearance was reframed as evidence of political persecution, transforming Trump from a former president into a martyr for conservative causes. His fundraising surged with every legal setback, as supporters viewed donations as acts of resistance against what they perceived as a weaponized justice system. This victim narrative became central to his political identity, preparing the ground for how he would later interpret and exploit the assassination attempt.

Trump's landslide in the primary was the product of a strategy honed by his two campaign managers: Susie Wiles and Chris LaCivita. The MAGA base was strong enough to assure Trump's victory in the

GOP primaries, they concluded, giving them time to test-run a plan to defeat Biden in November. His primary opponents, including Florida Governor Ron DeSantis, never managed to present a compelling alternative vision that could compete with Trump's combination of grievance politics and promises of retribution. By the time the general election campaign began in earnest, Trump had successfully consolidated Republican support and was positioned to present himself as the inevitable nominee of a party that had been completely remade in his image.

The Stakes of the 2024 Election

The 2024 presidential election was widely understood by both parties as a potentially decisive moment for American democracy, with each side viewing the other's victory as an existential threat to the republic. Trump's political movement was seen by some historians and some former Trump administrators as authoritarian, while the campaign made false and misleading statements, including claims of electoral fraud in 2020. Democrats painted the election as a choice between democracy and authoritarianism, warning that Trump's return would mean the end of constitutional governance and the rule of law.

Republicans, meanwhile, framed the election as America's last chance to prevent socialist transformation and cultural destruction. They pointed to concerns about border security, crime rates, and what they saw as the weaponization of government institutions against conservatives as evidence that Democratic control represented an existential threat to traditional American values. Voters felt that they were better off four years ago than they were today, with inflation and economic anxieties providing concrete reasons for political change beyond ideological considerations.

The international stakes were equally high, with allies and adversaries alike closely watching whether American democracy could produce stable leadership or would continue the pattern of dramatic policy reversals with each change of administration. Trump laid out a second-term agenda that would reshape America and its role in the world, including imposing harsh abortion restrictions, gutting environmental protections, and placing the entire federal bureaucracy under presidential control. The election represented not just a choice between candidates, but between fundamentally different visions of what America should be and how it should engage with the world. In this high-stakes environment, the margin for error was virtually nonexistent, and the potential for post-election conflict seemed almost guaranteed regardless of who won. It was into this powder keg that the events of July 13th would explode, transforming an already consequential election into something that would be remembered as a turning point in American political history.

CHAPTER 2: SECURITY CONCERNS AND EARLY WARNINGS

In the months leading up to July 13, 2024, a complex web of intelligence reports, resource constraints, and bureaucratic failures was quietly building toward what would become the most significant Secret Service failure since the attempted assassination of President Ronald Reagan in 1981. Behind the scenes, federal agencies were tracking multiple credible threats against Donald Trump's life, including sophisticated plots orchestrated by foreign adversaries and domestic extremists. Yet despite these mounting dangers, the very agency charged with protecting presidential candidates was systematically denying requests for enhanced security measures, citing budget constraints and personnel limitations that would prove catastrophically inadequate when the moment of crisis arrived.

The warning signs were everywhere for those willing to see them. Intelligence reports flowing into the Secret Service painted a picture of an unprecedented threat environment, where traditional security protocols designed for a different era were proving insufficient against modern dangers. Social media platforms were amplifying violent rhetoric to massive audiences, while foreign adversaries were actively plotting to eliminate American political leaders. Domestic terrorist organizations were proliferating, and the accessibility of military-grade weapons made every public appearance a potential target. Yet the institutional response was marked by denial, delay, and dangerous complacency that would have deadly consequences in the fields of Butler County, Pennsylvania.

Intelligence Reports on Iranian Threats

The Islamic Revolutionary Guard Corps had been actively plotting to assassinate Donald Trump since his presidency, when he ordered the killing of Iranian military commander Qasem Soleimani in 2020. By 2024, these threats had evolved from rhetorical bluster into concrete operational planning, with Iranian agents recruiting American assets to carry out attacks on U.S. soil. The Secret Service had increased Trump's security detail in recent weeks because of intelligence indicating that Iran was plotting to assassinate him, representing a clear escalation in the threat profile that should have triggered maximum protective measures.

Just one day after the Butler shooting, a Pakistani man named Asif Merchant, reported to be an agent of the Islamic Revolutionary Guard Corps, was arrested for a separate plot to kill Trump at a rally. Merchant paid $5,000 to federal agents posing as hired assassins and told them they would receive their instructions after he had left the country. This parallel Iranian operation, unconnected to Thomas Matthew Crooks, demonstrated the sophisticated and multi-pronged nature of foreign threats against American political figures. The timing was not coincidental—Iranian intelligence had clearly identified the 2024 campaign period as an optimal window for eliminating Trump.

Intelligence assessments warned that Iranian operatives were specifically targeting outdoor rallies as vulnerable points in Trump's security envelope. These reports detailed how foreign adversaries viewed large, public campaign events as presenting the best opportunities for successful attacks, given the logistical challenges of securing expansive perimeters and screening thousands of attendees. The intelligence was specific, credible, and urgent—

15

exactly the type of threat information that should have prompted immediate security enhancements and revised protective protocols for all outdoor campaign events.

Secret Service Resource Denials

Despite mounting intelligence about Iranian assassination plots and increased domestic threats, the Secret Service repeatedly denied requests from Trump's protective detail for additional resources throughout the 2024 campaign. A disturbing pattern emerged of the agency's headquarters systematically rejecting requests for enhanced counter drone systems, counter assault team personnel, and counter snipers that could have prevented or mitigated the Butler attack. These denials weren't based on threat assessments or security analysis, but rather on budgetary constraints and bureaucratic resistance to expanding protection for a former president seeking office again.

The Secret Service's own internal communications, revealed through congressional investigation, showed a "history of denials" to requests for additional security assets during Trump's campaign. Specifically concerning the Butler rally, enhanced counter drone systems were requested but not provided, despite intelligence indicating increased risks at outdoor events. Counter assault teams, specialized units designed to respond to active threats, were similarly denied despite repeated requests from agents on Trump's detail who understood the escalating danger environment better than headquarters bureaucrats.

On July 9, 2024, just four days before Butler, Trump's rally in Doral lacked countersnipers even after a briefing the day before from the Secret Service Protective Intelligence Division led to the determination that counter snipers should be present at all of Trump's outdoor rallies due to intelligence reflecting increased risks. This represented a stunning failure of institutional communication and resource allocation, where life-or-death security decisions were being made based on administrative convenience rather than threat reality. The agents closest to Trump knew what was needed to keep him safe, but the agency's leadership consistently chose cost-cutting over comprehensive protection.

The Growing Threat Environment

By 2024, the threat landscape facing American political figures had fundamentally transformed from anything the Secret Service had previously encountered. Traditional models of presidential protection, developed during the Cold War era of state-to-state conflict, were proving inadequate against a new matrix of dangers that included foreign intelligence operations, domestic terrorism, lone wolf attackers, and the viral spread of violent rhetoric through social media platforms that could radicalize individuals in real-time. The service was fighting twenty-first century threats with twentieth century protocols, creating dangerous gaps that sophisticated adversaries were learning to exploit.

Social media algorithms were amplifying the most extreme voices while creating echo chambers that reinforced the belief that political violence was not just acceptable but necessary. The January 6th Capitol attack had shattered longstanding taboos against political violence, demonstrating to potential attackers that direct assaults on democratic institutions were possible and might even be celebrated

17

by large segments of the population. This normalization of political violence created a permission structure for would-be assassins who could envision themselves as heroes rather than criminals.

The accessibility of military-grade weapons and tactical training meant that individual attackers could now pose threats previously associated only with terrorist organizations or state actors. Thomas Matthew Crooks's ability to position himself on a rooftop with an AR-15-style rifle and engage a presidential candidate from 130 yards demonstrated how readily available technology and weapons had democratized the capacity for political assassination. The Secret Service's threat assessment models had not adequately adapted to this new reality, where single individuals with modest resources could pose existential threats to the continuity of American democracy.

Warning Signs Ignored

The most tragic aspect of the Butler assassination attempt was how preventable it should have been given the numerous warning signs that preceded it. Local law enforcement had identified the building where Crooks positioned himself as a potential security vulnerability during advance planning, yet no agent was posted there on the day of the rally. Counter-sniper teams that could have detected and neutralized the threat were available but not deployed due to resource constraints that prioritized cost savings over comprehensive protection. Communication systems between local and federal law enforcement were fragmented, creating dangerous information gaps that allowed the attacker to operate undetected.

The Secret Service agent tasked with leading communications at Butler—the "security room agent"—was assigned the role only two days before the rally and discovered the existence of a second command post only after overhearing conversations between Pennsylvania State Police officers. This represented a fundamental breakdown in security planning, where critical coordination responsibilities were assigned to personnel unfamiliar with local arrangements and communication protocols. Such last-minute assignments violated basic security principles that had been developed through decades of hard-won experience protecting American leaders.

Perhaps most damning was the lack of structured communication between agencies, which investigators later identified as likely the greatest contributor to the Secret Service failures at Butler. The fragmented command structure meant that when local law enforcement spotted suspicious activity around Crooks's position, this information never reached the agents directly protecting Trump. Critical intelligence about potential threats was trapped in bureaucratic silos at the precise moment when rapid coordination could have saved lives. These weren't technical failures or resource limitations—they were preventable organizational breakdowns that created the precise conditions for assassination attempts to succeed.

CHAPTER 3: THE BUTLER RALLY - SETTING THE STAGE

The decision to hold a campaign rally in Butler, Pennsylvania, on July 13, 2024, seemed routine enough—just another stop in the endless cycle of speeches, crowds, and media coverage that defines modern presidential campaigns. The Butler Farm Show Grounds offered the perfect venue for Trump's signature outdoor rallies: expansive fields that could accommodate thousands of supporters, ample parking for the MAGA faithful who would drive hours to attend, and the kind of rural, working-class setting where Trump's populist message resonated most powerfully. Located in a county that had voted overwhelmingly for Trump in both 2016 and 2020, Butler represented friendly territory where the candidate could energize his base while generating the kind of massive crowd footage that dominated social media and reinforced his narrative of unstoppable momentum.

Yet beneath the familiar pageantry of American campaign politics, a more complex and ultimately deadly drama was unfolding. The choice of Butler wasn't just about politics—it was about Pennsylvania's nineteen electoral votes and the mathematical reality that no Republican had won the presidency without carrying the Keystone State since 1988. As advance teams began setting up generators and staging areas three days before the rally, a web of security preparations, bureaucratic failures, and pure chance was converging toward eight seconds of gunfire that would change American history. The stage was being set not just for another Trump rally, but for the most consequential moment of the entire 2024 election.

Pennsylvania: The Ultimate Swing State

Pennsylvania represented the crown jewel of American swing states in 2024, with its nineteen electoral votes offering any candidate a decisive advantage in the race to 270. The state had swung from Trump in 2016 to Biden in 2020 by razor-thin margins, making it the ultimate bellwether for national political sentiment and the most closely watched battleground in the entire election. Trump's campaign recognized that their path back to the White House ran directly through Pennsylvania's industrial cities, suburban counties, and rural townships, where economic anxiety and cultural grievances had created a volatile political landscape that could swing either way depending on turnout and messaging.

The rally was part of the campaign's systematic attempts to garner votes in Pennsylvania, a swing state that both parties understood would likely determine the election outcome. Butler County itself epitomized the kind of territory where Trump excelled—predominantly white, working-class communities that had been economically disrupted by globalization and felt left behind by cultural changes sweeping urban America. These voters had powered Trump's surprise victory in 2016 and remained essential to his coalition, but they also represented the kind of swing voters who could be persuaded by the right message or motivated by the right moment.

Beyond electoral mathematics, Pennsylvania held deep symbolic significance for Trump's narrative of American restoration. The state's industrial heritage, from Pittsburgh's steel mills to the oil refineries of western counties, embodied the working-class prosperity that Trump promised to restore through his "America First" policies. Choosing Butler for a major rally sent a clear message that Trump remained committed to the forgotten Americans who had first elevated him to power, while also demonstrating his confidence in reclaiming states that had slipped away in 2020.

Planning the July 13th Rally

The Trump campaign announced the Butler rally on July 3, 2024, giving the advance team just ten days to coordinate what would become one of the most scrutinized events in American political history. The Butler Farm Show Grounds in Connoquenessing Township and Meridian offered the ideal setting for Trump's preferred rally format—an outdoor venue where massive crowds could create the visual spectacle that had become central to his political brand. The site's open fields could accommodate thousands of supporters while providing the kind of authentic, rural American backdrop that resonated with Trump's base and dominated media coverage.

On July 10, an advance team began setting up for the rally, including the installation of generators in a large open field and the construction of the stage platform where Trump would deliver his remarks. The planning process involved coordination between the Trump campaign, Secret Service, local law enforcement, and venue management to ensure smooth logistics for what was expected to be a crowd of over 8,000 people. Dave McCormick, the Republican nominee in Pennsylvania's concurrent U.S. Senate election, was invited to appear onstage during the rally to increase support for his campaign, making the event part of a broader Republican strategy to reclaim control of both the presidency and Senate.

The Federal Bureau of Investigation had no information about any particular threats before the incident, which contributed to what would later be identified as dangerous complacency in security planning. The routine nature of the planning process—treating Butler as just another campaign stop rather than a high-risk event requiring maximum security—reflected the institutional blind spots that made the assassination attempt possible. Critical decisions about perimeter security, building coverage, and communication protocols were made based on standard procedures rather than the heightened threat environment that intelligence reports had identified.

Security Preparations and Failures

The security preparations for the Butler rally revealed a catastrophic series of institutional failures that transformed what should have been routine protection into a near-fatal vulnerability. Local law enforcement had identified the building where Thomas Matthew Crooks would position himself as a potential security concern during advance planning, yet no agent was posted there on the day of the rally. The building, located just 130 yards from the stage, offered a clear line of sight to Trump's position and should have been either secured or continuously monitored throughout the event.

The Secret Service's reliance on local law enforcement to secure the perimeter created dangerous gaps in coverage and communication that the attacker exploited. The Butler rally was the first time a former president and candidate had received countersnipers from the Secret Service, bucking tradition, yet these teams were not adequately briefed about the elevated threat environment leading up to the rally. The lack of structured communication was likely the greatest contributor to the failures of the Secret Service at Butler, with separate command posts for local and federal law enforcement creating information silos at the moment when coordination was most critical.

Perhaps most damning was the assignment of the security room agent—responsible for leading communications—only two days before the rally. This agent, from the Secret Service's Buffalo field office, discovered the existence of the second command post only after overhearing conversations between Pennsylvania State Police officers stationed in the Secret Service's command post. Such last-minute personnel assignments violated basic security protocols and ensured that critical coordination functions would be performed by someone unfamiliar with local arrangements and communication systems.

The Crowd Gathers

As the afternoon of July 13th progressed, thousands of Trump supporters began streaming toward the Butler Farm Show Grounds, creating the kind of massive, enthusiastic crowd that had become the hallmark of Trump rallies throughout his political career. Red MAGA hats dotted the landscape as families, retirees, and working-class Americans made their way through security checkpoints and into the sprawling field where the stage awaited. Many had driven hours to attend, viewing the rally not just as a political event but as a celebration of shared values and a demonstration of support for a candidate they saw as uniquely capable of defending their way of life.

The crowd of approximately 8,000 people represented a cross-section of Trump's Pennsylvania coalition—farmers and factory workers, small business owners and retirees, military veterans and their families. They came despite the summer heat and the long wait times, motivated by a sense of political urgency and personal connection to Trump that transcended typical campaign enthusiasm. For many attendees, this would be their first opportunity to see Trump in person since his presidency, making the event feel like a reunion as much as a political rally.

Among the crowd was 50-year-old Corey Comperatore, a volunteer firefighter and devoted family man who had brought his wife and daughters to share in what they expected to be an inspiring evening of politics and patriotism. Comperatore embodied the kind of working-class American that Trump's message was designed to reach—a man who served his community, loved his country, and believed that Trump represented the best hope for preserving the America he had grown up in. None of the 8,000 people gathering in that Pennsylvania field could have imagined that they were about to witness an assassination attempt, or that one of their own would make the ultimate sacrifice protecting his family from a gunman's bullets.

CHAPTER 4: 6:11 PM

At exactly 6:11 PM on July 13, 2024, the trajectory of American politics changed forever in eight seconds of gunfire that transformed a routine campaign rally into the most significant assassination attempt in over four decades. Donald Trump had been speaking for just eight minutes, gesticulating toward an immigration chart behind him, when the sharp crack of rifle fire shattered the summer evening air. In those terrifying moments, as chaos erupted across the Butler Farm Show Grounds and Secret Service agents rushed the stage, the thin line between democracy and tragedy was measured in millimeters. A single bullet, fired from an AR-15-style rifle by a 20-year-old would-be assassin, grazed Trump's right ear and missed ending his life by the smallest possible margin.

What happened next would define not just the remainder of the 2024 campaign, but Trump's entire political legacy. As Secret Service agents swarmed around the wounded former president, urging him to evacuate immediately, Trump made a decision that defied both protocol and human instinct. Rising from behind the podium where he had taken cover, blood streaming down the right side of his face, he thrust his fist into the air and delivered three words that would echo through the rest of the election: "Fight! Fight! Fight!" In those eight seconds, a campaign rally became a moment of historical consequence, a presidential candidate became a symbol of survival, and American politics entered uncharted territory from which it would never return.

Thomas Matthew Crooks: Profile of a Shooter

Thomas Matthew Crooks was an unlikely assassin whose motivations remain a mystery even after extensive FBI investigation. The 20-year-old nursing home worker from Bethel Park, Pennsylvania, lived a seemingly ordinary life that provided few clues about his decision to attempt political murder. Investigators found that he had searched for images of Trump, Biden, and several other public figures, suggesting his interest in political violence wasn't specifically partisan but rather opportunistic. His online activity revealed searches about major depressive disorder, though there has been no determination about whether he was formally diagnosed with mental illness.

The most chilling detail investigators uncovered was Crooks's research into historical assassinations. On July 6, just one week before the Butler rally, he searched for "how far was Oswald away from Kennedy," referencing the assassination of John F. Kennedy and suggesting he was studying assassination techniques. That same day, he registered for Trump's rally, indicating his attack was planned at least a week in advance. Two hours before the assassination attempt, Crooks flew a drone near the rally site, conducting reconnaissance that should have been detected by security systems.

Crooks's ability to position himself on the roof of a building just 130 yards from Trump's stage revealed how readily available technology and weapons had democratized the capacity for political assassination. Armed with an AR-15-style rifle and basic tactical knowledge, this unremarkable young man nearly changed the course of American history. His death at the hands of Secret Service snipers twelve seconds after opening fire ensured that his true motivations would die with him, leaving investigators and the public to grapple with the disturbing reality that political violence could emerge from the most unexpected sources.

The Eight Seconds That Changed History

The assassination attempt unfolded with terrifying speed and precision that exposed every vulnerability in the security apparatus protecting America's political leaders. At 6:11 PM, as Trump pointed toward the immigration chart behind him, Crooks fired eight rounds in rapid succession from his position on the AGR International building. The first shot missed Trump's head by approximately two inches, grazing his right ear and sending him immediately to the ground behind the protective lectern. Four seconds after Crooks began firing, Aaron Zaliponi, a member of the Butler County Emergency Service Unit, shot at the assassin and hit his rifle, preventing him from firing additional rounds at the wounded former president.

The crowd's reaction was a mixture of confusion, terror, and disbelief as the reality of what was happening slowly penetrated the summer evening atmosphere. Many attendees initially thought the sounds were fireworks or mechanical failures rather than gunshots, but the sight of Trump dropping behind the podium and Secret Service agents rushing the stage made the deadly nature of the situation unmistakably clear. Screams and shouts filled the air as thousands of people simultaneously realized they were witnessing an assassination attempt in real time.

Twelve seconds after the shooting began, Crooks was shot and killed by the United States Secret Service Counter Sniper Team, ending the immediate threat but beginning a political earthquake that would reshape the entire election. Those eight seconds contained enough violence and drama to fill a Hollywood thriller, but their political consequences would prove far more significant than their brief duration might suggest. In less time than it takes to read this paragraph, American democracy had been tested by its oldest enemy—political violence—and the outcome would reverberate through every remaining day of the 2024 campaign.

"Fight, Fight, Fight!" - Trump's Defiant Response

What happened next transformed Donald Trump from assassination target into political legend. As Secret Service agents formed a protective circle around the wounded former president, their immediate priority was evacuation—getting him off the stage and away from potential additional threats as quickly as possible. Standard protocol called for rapid, low-profile extraction to minimize exposure time and avoid providing additional targets for other possible shooters. But Trump, with blood streaming down his face and his ear damaged by the bullet's impact, had different instincts about how this moment should be remembered.

Instead of allowing agents to immediately escort him to safety, Trump insisted on standing up and facing the crowd that had just witnessed his near-death experience. In conversations with multiple Trump campaign officials and advisers in the following weeks, they learned that the president later remarked to his close allies that he knew in that moment he needed to leave his supporters with a potent image. Trump, who has long fixated on projecting a portrait of strength, did not want the assassination attempt to leave him looking weak or defeated by the attack.

Rising slowly from behind the podium, Trump thrust his fist through the agents swarming around him and pumped it toward the crowd while shouting "Fight! Fight! Fight!" The image captured by Associated Press photographer Evan Vucci—a bloodied but defiant Trump, fist raised against the backdrop of the American flag, surrounded by Secret Service agents—would become one of the most powerful political photographs in modern American history. In that single moment, Trump transformed himself from victim to victor, from target to symbol, from wounded politician to martyred leader who had literally shed blood for his cause.

Corey Comperatore: The Hero Who Died

Among the 8,000 people who came to Butler that evening to hear Donald Trump speak, none embodied the values of service and sacrifice more than Corey Comperatore, a 50-year-old volunteer firefighter who had brought his wife and two daughters to share what they expected to be an inspiring evening of politics and patriotism. Comperatore represented the heart of Trump's Pennsylvania coalition—a working-class man who served his community through decades of volunteer firefighting, loved his family deeply, and believed in the vision of America that Trump promised to restore. He was exactly the kind of forgotten American that Trump's populist message was designed to reach and protect.

When the gunshots rang out across the Butler Farm Show Grounds, Comperatore's instincts as both a first responder and a father took over immediately. Rather than diving for cover or running from the danger, he threw himself over his wife and daughters, shielding them with his own body from the rifle fire that was raining down from Crooks's position. The bullet that killed Comperatore was intended for Trump, but this devoted family man intercepted it with his life, becoming both a victim of political violence and a hero who died protecting the people he loved most.

Comperatore's death transformed him into a symbol of the stakes involved in American political life and the price that ordinary citizens sometimes pay for the extremism that has infected democratic discourse. His sacrifice would be remembered and honored throughout the remainder of the campaign, with Trump frequently referencing the firefighter's heroism as evidence of the character and courage of his supporters. The tragedy of Comperatore's death—a man who came to hear a political speech and died protecting his family from an assassin's bullet—captured the senseless nature of political violence and its impact on innocent Americans who simply wanted to participate in democratic life.

CHAPTER 5: CHAOS AND HEROISM

In the immediate aftermath of the gunshots that shattered the summer evening in Butler, Pennsylvania, the true test of America's protective systems began. What followed those eight seconds of rifle fire was a complex drama of institutional response, individual heroism, and organizational failure that would be dissected and analyzed for years to come. Secret Service agents who had trained their entire careers for this exact moment found themselves navigating not just an active shooter situation, but a chaotic environment where communication systems failed, coordination broke down, and split-second decisions meant the difference between life and death for thousands of people.

Yet amid the institutional failures and bureaucratic breakdowns, extraordinary acts of courage and professionalism prevented what could have been a far greater tragedy. Local law enforcement officers, rally attendees, and medical personnel responded with the kind of selfless bravery that defines the best of American character. Their actions in those critical minutes—as confusion reigned and the full scope of the threat remained unknown—demonstrated that even when systems fail, individual Americans can rise to meet the most demanding challenges. The story of those chaotic minutes is simultaneously one of institutional inadequacy and personal heroism, revealing both the vulnerabilities and the resilience that characterize American democracy under extreme stress.

Secret Service Response and Failures

The Secret Service's response to the assassination attempt revealed both the agency's tactical professionalism and its systemic vulnerabilities in ways that would reshape presidential protection forever. Within seconds of the first shot, agents moved with practiced precision to shield Trump's body and create a protective barrier around him, demonstrating the kind of selfless courage that defines their mission. The Counter Sniper Team's elimination of Thomas Matthew Crooks just twelve seconds after he began firing prevented additional casualties and ended the immediate threat with remarkable speed and accuracy.

However, the agency's performance also exposed critical failures that had been building for months before Butler. The most significant breakdown occurred in the communication systems that should have coordinated the response between local and federal law enforcement. The Secret Service had established separate command posts from local authorities, creating information silos that prevented crucial intelligence about Crooks's suspicious behavior from reaching the agents directly protecting Trump. When local officers spotted the gunman on the roof, this vital information never made it to the protective detail until shots had already been fired.

The incident represented the most significant security failure by the Secret Service since the attempted assassination of President Ronald Reagan in 1981, forcing a comprehensive reevaluation of protective protocols and resource allocation. Director Kimberly Cheatle faced bipartisan calls for her resignation when she testified before the United States House Committee on Oversight and Accountability on July 22, stepping down the following day. The agency's failures at Butler would ultimately lead to six personnel facing disciplinary action, though investigators concluded that the penalties received were too weak to match the severity of the institutional breakdowns that nearly cost a former president his life.

Local Law Enforcement's Actions

Local law enforcement's performance during the Butler assassination attempt represented a mixture of individual heroism and systemic coordination failures that illustrated both the strengths and weaknesses of multi-agency security operations. Pennsylvania State Police and Butler County officers had been assigned to secure the perimeter around the rally site, including the building where Crooks ultimately positioned himself. Several officers had actually spotted suspicious activity around the shooter's location and attempted to investigate, but their findings never reached the Secret Service agents protecting Trump due to the fragmented communication systems.

The most dramatic moment of local law enforcement response came when Aaron Zaliponi, a member of the Butler County Emergency Service Unit, engaged Crooks just four seconds after the shooting began. Zaliponi's quick thinking and accurate shooting hit the assassin's rifle, preventing him from firing additional rounds at Trump and the crowd. This split-second intervention likely saved multiple lives and demonstrated the kind of rapid response that effective security coordination should enable. Local officers also played crucial roles in crowd control and evacuation, preventing panic from turning into stampede conditions that could have caused additional casualties.

However, the investigation revealed that local law enforcement had identified the AGR International building as a potential security vulnerability during advance planning, yet no continuous monitoring was established for the location. The building offered a clear line of sight to Trump's position and should have been either secured or under constant surveillance throughout the event. The

34

failure to maintain eyes on this obvious threat location represented a fundamental breakdown in security planning that created the window of opportunity Crooks exploited. Despite these systemic failures, individual officers performed with courage and professionalism when the crisis began, demonstrating that personal heroism can sometimes compensate for institutional inadequacies.

The Crowd's Reaction

The reaction of the 8,000 Trump supporters packed into the Butler Farm Show Grounds revealed both the terror and resilience of ordinary Americans confronted with extraordinary violence. Initial confusion dominated the first seconds after gunfire erupted, with many attendees thinking the sounds were fireworks, mechanical failures, or audio feedback rather than rifle shots. The summer evening atmosphere and festive mood of the rally made the reality of an assassination attempt almost impossible to process immediately, creating a brief moment of stunned disbelief before panic began to set in.

As the situation became clear—Trump dropping behind the podium, Secret Service agents rushing the stage, screams and shouts filling the air—the crowd's response evolved from confusion to terror to protective instincts. Many attendees threw themselves to the ground or sought cover behind bleachers and barriers, while others began pushing toward exits in what could have become a deadly stampede. Parents grabbed children, elderly attendees sought help from younger rallygoers, and strangers began protecting strangers in displays of spontaneous solidarity that transcended political affiliation.

Perhaps most remarkably, many in the crowd remained focused on Trump's condition and safety even as their own lives were potentially at risk. When Trump rose from behind the podium with his fist raised, shouting "Fight! Fight! Fight!", a significant portion of the crowd responded with cheers and applause despite not knowing whether additional shooters might be present. This reaction demonstrated the deep emotional connection between Trump and his supporters, but also the dangerous willingness to prioritize political loyalty over personal safety that characterized the most devoted elements of his base. The crowd's behavior in those critical minutes—alternating between panic and defiance, fear and loyalty—captured the complex psychology of American political tribalism under extreme stress.

Medical Response and Evacuation

The medical response to the Butler assassination attempt showcased both the preparedness of emergency personnel and the challenges of providing care in an active threat environment. Trump's visible injury—blood streaming from his damaged right ear—required immediate assessment and treatment, but Secret Service protocols demanded rapid evacuation from the scene before comprehensive medical care could be provided. The tension between medical needs and security requirements created difficult decisions about how to balance Trump's health against continued exposure to potential additional threats.

On-site medical personnel quickly established that Trump's injury, while dramatic in appearance, was not life-threatening. The bullet had grazed his upper right ear rather than penetrating deeper tissue, avoiding damage to critical structures while creating the kind of bleeding head wound that appears far more serious than it actually is. This rapid medical assessment allowed security personnel to proceed with evacuation procedures without the complications that would have accompanied a more severe injury requiring immediate surgical intervention.

Trump was taken to a nearby hospital where he was treated and released later that evening, with medical staff confirming that his injuries were indeed minor despite their dramatic appearance. The hospital visit served multiple purposes—ensuring comprehensive medical evaluation, providing time for security personnel to assess ongoing threats, and offering Trump's team the opportunity to craft their narrative response to the attack. Two days later, Trump made his first public appearance at the 2024 Republican National Convention in Milwaukee, Wisconsin, wearing a bandage on his ear that became an iconic symbol of his survival and resilience. The medical response's efficiency and professionalism ensured that what could have been a fatal attack became instead a survivable injury that Trump would transform into political advantage.

CHAPTER 6: THE ICONIC IMAGE

In the annals of American political photography, certain images transcend their immediate context to become defining symbols of entire historical moments. Abraham Lincoln's weathered face during the Civil War, Franklin Roosevelt's confident smile during the Great Depression, John F. Kennedy's youthful vigor during the Cold War—these photographs capture not just individual leaders, but the spirit of their times. On July 13, 2024, Associated Press photographer Evan Vucci captured what would instantly join this pantheon of iconic American political imagery: Donald Trump, bloodied but defiant, fist raised against the backdrop of the American flag, surrounded by Secret Service agents in the immediate aftermath of an assassination attempt.

The photograph's power lay not just in its dramatic composition, but in its perfect encapsulation of Trump's political brand and the moment's historic significance. Here was visual proof of Trump's survival, his defiance, and his unbreakable connection to American symbolism, all captured in a single frame that would be shared millions of times within hours and studied by historians for generations. The image transformed what could have been a story of victimization into a narrative of triumph, providing Trump's campaign with the most powerful piece of political messaging imaginable—authentic documentation of his literal willingness to bleed for his cause.

Blood, Fist, and Flag

The visual elements that made Vucci's photograph so powerful were almost impossibly perfect in their symbolic alignment with Trump's political messaging. The blood streaming down Trump's face provided undeniable evidence of the reality and severity of the attack, while simultaneously evoking the sacrifice and suffering that Trump claimed to endure on behalf of his supporters. This wasn't staged political theater or campaign propaganda—it was authentic documentation of a man who had literally shed blood while fighting for his political beliefs, creating a level of credibility that no amount of campaign spending could purchase.

Trump's raised fist, thrust defiantly toward the crowd despite his injury and the ongoing security threat, captured the essence of his political brand in a single gesture. The fist represented strength, defiance, and refusal to be intimidated by enemies—themes that had defined Trump's political career from his first campaign through his presidency and into his comeback attempt. The gesture was simultaneously one of victory and resistance, suggesting both triumph over the attack and determination to continue fighting despite the danger.

The American flag fluttering behind Trump in the photograph provided the perfect patriotic backdrop that transformed a moment of violence into a tableau of American resilience. The flag's position—directly behind the wounded but unbowed candidate—created visual symbolism that linked Trump's survival to the survival of America itself. The three elements—blood, fist, and flag—combined to create an image that told a complete story without requiring any explanatory text: here was an American leader who had been attacked by enemies but refused to surrender, standing bloodied but unbroken beneath the symbol of the nation he sought to lead.

Evan Vucci's Pulitzer-Worthy Photograph

Evan Vucci's positioning and instincts as a photojournalist allowed him to capture what many already consider one of the most important news photographs of the decade. As an Associated Press photographer covering the Trump rally, Vucci was positioned with other media personnel in the designated press area when the shooting began. While many journalists and photographers understandably sought cover when gunfire erupted, Vucci maintained his professional focus and continued shooting even as chaos unfolded around him, recognizing that he was witnessing a moment of extraordinary historical significance that demanded documentation.

The technical excellence of the photograph—its sharp focus, perfect composition, and dramatic lighting—demonstrated Vucci's skill and experience in capturing breaking news under the most challenging circumstances. The image shows Trump in perfect clarity despite the movement and confusion surrounding him, with the American flag positioned ideally in the background and the Secret Service agents arranged in a way that frames rather than obscures the central figure. This level of compositional perfection, achieved in seconds during a life-threatening situation, represents photojournalism at its absolute finest.

Within hours of the photograph's release, media critics and photography experts were comparing it to the most famous images in American political history. The photograph possessed the rare combination of technical excellence, dramatic content, and historical significance that defines award-winning photojournalism. Industry observers immediately began speculating about Pulitzer Prize recognition, understanding that Vucci had captured not just a news event, but a moment that would be studied and remembered long after the 2024 election was over. The image joined the ranks of photographs that don't just document history—they help shape it.

The Power of Visual Symbolism

The immediate impact of Vucci's photograph demonstrated the unique power of visual imagery to shape political narratives in ways that words alone cannot achieve. Within minutes of its publication, the image was being shared across social media platforms by Trump supporters who saw it as definitive proof of their candidate's courage, strength, and divine protection. The photograph provided visual validation of the narrative that Trump had been constructing throughout his political career—that he was a fighter who would never surrender, even when facing mortal danger.

The image's symbolic power extended far beyond Trump's existing base of support, reaching Americans who might have been skeptical of his political messaging but could not deny the authenticity of his response to an assassination attempt. The photograph showed, rather than claimed, Trump's resilience under fire, providing evidence that even his critics had to acknowledge. This visual proof of Trump's behavior in a moment of genuine crisis carried more persuasive weight than any campaign advertisement or political speech could have achieved.

Political scientists and communications experts immediately recognized the photograph's potential to reshape the entire election narrative. The image transformed Trump from a controversial political figure into a symbol of American strength and determination, providing his campaign with messaging opportunities that extended far beyond the immediate aftermath of the assassination attempt. The photograph would appear on campaign merchandise, in political advertisements, and in supporter-generated content throughout the remainder of the election, serving as a constant reminder of Trump's survival and the idea that he was destined to lead America through its challenges.

Social Media Explosion

The viral spread of Vucci's photograph across social media platforms demonstrated the incredible speed with which powerful images can dominate global conversation in the digital age. Within minutes of the Associated Press releasing the photograph, it was being shared thousands of times per minute across Twitter, Facebook, Instagram, and other platforms. Trump supporters immediately embraced the image as proof of their candidate's divine protection and unbreakable spirit, while even some critics acknowledged the photograph's dramatic power and historical significance.

The image's virality was amplified by its perfect suitability for social media sharing—the photograph required no context or explanation to convey its meaning, making it ideal for platforms where users scroll quickly through content. Memes, variations, and artistic interpretations of the photograph began appearing within hours, as creative users found new ways to leverage its symbolic power. The image transcended typical political content by appealing to basic human emotions—admiration for courage under fire, respect for survival against odds, and appreciation for authentic leadership in crisis.

Perhaps most significantly, the photograph's social media dominance occurred organically, without paid promotion or campaign intervention. The image spread because users genuinely wanted to share it, creating the kind of authentic viral moment that campaigns spend millions trying to manufacture artificially. This organic virality gave the photograph additional credibility and impact, as audiences understood they were seeing genuine grassroots enthusiasm rather than purchased political messaging. The social media explosion around Vucci's photograph provided Trump's campaign with millions of dollars worth of free publicity and reinforced the narrative that his survival represented a moment of genuine historical importance that Americans instinctively recognized and celebrated.

CHAPTER 7: THE NATION RESPONDS

The immediate aftermath of the assassination attempt created a rare moment of national unity as Americans across the political spectrum reacted with shock, horror, and relief that Donald Trump had survived. Within hours of the shooting, political leaders from both parties issued statements condemning political violence and expressing gratitude that the attack had not succeeded. For a brief moment, the familiar patterns of partisan warfare gave way to something approaching the shared values and common decency that had once defined American political discourse, as even Trump's harshest critics acknowledged that assassination attempts have no place in democratic society.

Yet even as calls for unity echoed across the political landscape, the underlying tensions that had made such violence possible remained largely unaddressed. The assassination attempt became both a moment of reflection about the dangers of political extremism and a new source of partisan conflict over responsibility, security failures, and the appropriate response to political violence. Media coverage ranged from calls for introspection about heated rhetoric to immediate speculation about electoral implications, while international observers watched with concern about the stability of American democracy. The nation's response revealed both its capacity for moments of unity and its inability to escape the deeper divisions that continued to threaten its democratic foundations.

Biden's Call for Unity

President Joe Biden's response to the assassination attempt demonstrated both presidential leadership and the complex political dynamics surrounding his relationship with Trump. Within hours of the shooting, Biden delivered a brief press conference where he condemned the violence and expressed sympathy to his opponent, notably calling him "Donald" in a rare break from the animosity between the two men. This gesture of personal concern transcended their political rivalry and reflected the gravity of the moment, acknowledging that some threats are larger than partisan competition.

Biden's shooting response allowed him to look presidential and serve as the 'consoler-in-chief', a role that sitting presidents traditionally fill during national crises. He delivered a short speech from the Oval Office on July 14, urging Americans to 'lower the temperature in our politics' and resolve their differences peacefully rather than through violence. The president's measured tone and call for national reflection represented the kind of unifying leadership that Americans expect during moments of crisis, regardless of party affiliation.

However, Biden's unity message faced immediate political challenges as some Trump supporters blamed the president's rhetoric for creating the atmosphere that led to the assassination attempt. The delicate balance between condemning violence and avoiding responsibility for the political climate proved difficult to maintain, particularly as the campaign continued and partisan tensions remained high. Despite Biden's sincere calls for de-escalation, the underlying political dynamics that had made violence possible remained largely unchanged, limiting the long-term impact of his presidential response.

Political Leaders' Statements

The bipartisan condemnation of the assassination attempt represented one of the few moments of genuine political unity during the deeply polarized 2024 election cycle. Republican leaders rallied around Trump with statements of support and gratitude for his survival, while also using the moment to criticize Democratic rhetoric they claimed had contributed to the violent political climate. House Speaker Mike Johnson and Senate Minority Leader Mitch McConnell issued strong statements condemning political violence while calling for investigations into the security failures that had allowed the attack to occur.

Democratic leaders faced a more complex challenge in crafting their responses, needing to condemn the violence while avoiding any appearance of sympathy for Trump's political positions. Former presidents Barack Obama and Bill Clinton, along with former Secretary of State Hillary Clinton, issued statements condemning the attack and wishing Trump a swift recovery. Nancy Pelosi, whose husband had been attacked by a politically motivated assailant, said "As one whose family has been the victim of political violence, I know firsthand that political violence of any kind has no place in our society."

The statements from political leaders revealed the difficulty of addressing political violence in a highly polarized environment where every response is scrutinized for partisan advantage. While the condemnations were largely genuine, they also became part of the ongoing political narrative, with each party using the moment to reinforce their preferred messages about responsibility, rhetoric, and the state of American democracy. The brief moment of unity proved fragile as normal political competition resumed within days of the shooting.

Media Coverage and Analysis

Media coverage of the assassination attempt revealed both the best and worst tendencies of American journalism under pressure. Initial reporting focused appropriately on the basic facts—Trump's condition, the shooter's identity, and the security failures that had allowed the attack to occur. Major news outlets demonstrated professionalism in avoiding speculation about motives while the investigation was ongoing and in emphasizing the seriousness of political violence regardless of partisan considerations.

However, the media's response also quickly turned to political analysis and electoral implications, with commentators immediately speculating about how the assassination attempt might affect Trump's polling numbers and campaign strategy. Some analysts drew comparisons to the 1981 attempted assassination of Ronald Reagan, which had boosted his approval ratings, while others questioned whether Trump would benefit similarly. This rapid pivot from news coverage to political analysis reflected the media's struggle to balance legitimate public interest in electoral implications with appropriate sensitivity to the gravity of political violence.

The coverage also revealed deep divides in how different media outlets and audiences interpreted the event's significance. Conservative media emphasized the heroism of Trump's response and questioned the security failures, while liberal outlets focused

47

more on the broader implications for political rhetoric and democratic norms. Social media platforms struggled to contain misinformation and conspiracy theories that emerged within hours of the shooting, demonstrating the challenges of maintaining accurate information during breaking news events. The media's handling of the assassination attempt became yet another source of partisan division rather than a unifying force for national reflection.

International Reactions

The international response to Trump's assassination attempt reflected global concerns about American political stability and the implications for international relations. Allied nations expressed relief at Trump's survival while privately worrying about what the attack revealed about the state of American democracy. Israeli Prime Minister Benjamin Netanyahu said he and his wife Sara were "shocked by the second assassination attempt against President Trump and were relieved to hear that it too failed," while noting that "we should not rely on luck" and hoping that measures would be taken to prevent future attacks.

European leaders, many of whom had complex relationships with Trump during his presidency, offered careful statements condemning political violence while avoiding commentary on American domestic politics. The assassination attempt reinforced concerns among traditional allies about American political stability and the potential for further violence during the election period. Some international observers drew parallels to political violence in developing democracies, expressing worry about whether American institutions remained strong enough to contain extremist threats.

Authoritarian leaders and America's adversaries watched the assassination attempt with different perspectives, seeing potential opportunities to exploit American political instability. The attack provided propaganda material for regimes that regularly criticized American democracy, allowing them to point to political violence as evidence of systemic problems in the American system. The international reaction demonstrated how domestic political violence in America has global implications, affecting everything from alliance relationships to international perceptions of American leadership and democratic values.

CHAPTER 8: CONSPIRACY THEORIES AND INVESTIGATIONS

Within hours of the assassination attempt, the information landscape surrounding July 13th became as chaotic and fragmented as the physical scene in Butler, Pennsylvania. Social media platforms exploded with competing narratives, alternative theories, and outright disinformation that threatened to overshadow the established facts of what had actually occurred. While law enforcement agencies began the painstaking work of investigating Thomas Matthew Crooks's background and motivations, online conspiracy theorists were already constructing elaborate alternative explanations that ranged from government cover-ups to staged political theater designed to boost Trump's electoral prospects.

The proliferation of misinformation created a parallel crisis that complicated both the official investigation and the public's understanding of events. As FBI agents collected evidence from the crime scene and Secret Service leadership faced mounting pressure to explain their failures, congressional leaders recognized that the assassination attempt demanded more than routine oversight—it required a comprehensive investigation that could restore public confidence in the agencies responsible for protecting American political leaders. The collision between official investigations and online speculation would define much of the public discourse surrounding the Butler shooting, revealing how difficult it had become to establish shared facts in an environment where every major event immediately spawns competing versions of reality.

Online Misinformation Spreads

The digital response to Trump's assassination attempt demonstrated the incredible speed with which misinformation can spread and take hold in the modern information environment. Within hours of the shooting, social media platforms were flooded with conspiracy theories ranging from claims that the attack was staged to allegations of government involvement in either facilitating or covering up the true scope of the plot. These theories gained traction partly because of legitimate questions about security failures, but also because of the deep distrust many Americans felt toward government institutions and mainstream media sources.

Conspiracy theorists seized on every gap in the initial reporting as evidence of deliberate deception, creating elaborate narratives that filled information voids with speculation and suspicion. The fact that Crooks's motivations remained unclear provided fertile ground for theories about hidden connections, secret handlers, and complex plots involving multiple perpetrators. Some online communities suggested the shooting was a "false flag" operation designed to generate sympathy for Trump, while others proposed that government agencies had deliberately allowed the attack to proceed as part of a broader conspiracy.

The viral nature of these conspiracy theories was amplified by social media algorithms that prioritized engagement over accuracy, ensuring that the most sensational and emotionally provocative content received the widest distribution. Platforms like Twitter, Facebook, and YouTube struggled to balance free speech concerns with the need to prevent the spread of dangerous misinformation that could incite additional violence or undermine legitimate investigations. The result was a information ecosystem where

51

conspiracy theories often traveled faster and reached more people than official statements from law enforcement agencies conducting the actual investigation.

FBI Investigation Begins

The FBI's investigation into the assassination attempt began immediately, with agents securing the crime scene and beginning the complex process of reconstructing Crooks's path to violence. Director Christopher Wray quickly established that the bureau would treat the shooting as both an assassination attempt and a domestic terrorism incident, bringing the full resources of federal law enforcement to bear on understanding how and why the attack had occurred. The investigation's scope extended far beyond the immediate crime scene to include Crooks's digital footprint, financial records, social connections, and any potential links to extremist organizations.

Mobile device forensics became a crucial element of the investigation as FBI Laboratory staff worked to defeat the security measures on Crooks's smartphones. Using advanced techniques, likely including Cellebrite devices or undisclosed in-house methods, investigators found that Crooks had searched for images of Trump, Biden, and several other public figures, suggesting his interest in political violence wasn't specifically partisan but rather opportunistic. The digital evidence revealed searches about major depressive disorder and the chilling July 6th query about "how far was Oswald away from Kennedy," referencing the assassination of John F. Kennedy.

The investigation faced unique challenges in determining motive, as Crooks's death at the scene eliminated the possibility of interrogation and confession. Without the perpetrator's own explanation for his actions, investigators had to rely on digital forensics, witness interviews, and behavioral analysis to construct a picture of what had driven a seemingly ordinary young man to attempt political murder. The FBI's methodical approach contrasted sharply with the immediate demands for answers from politicians and the public, creating tension between investigative thoroughness and political pressure for rapid conclusions.

Secret Service Director Resigns

The assassination attempt created an immediate crisis of confidence in Secret Service leadership that culminated in Director Kimberly Cheatle's resignation just ten days after the Butler shooting. Cheatle faced withering bipartisan criticism when she testified before the United States House Committee on Oversight and Accountability on July 22, as lawmakers from both parties demanded answers about how an armed assassin had been able to position himself on a rooftop with a clear line of sight to a former president. Her testimony, which many members found evasive and unsatisfactory, failed to restore confidence in the agency's ability to protect American political leaders.

The director's position became untenable as details emerged about the systematic resource denials and communication failures that had contributed to the assassination attempt's near success. Cheatle's claim that requests for additional security assets at the Butler rally had not been denied was contradicted by evidence showing a "history of denials" for enhanced security measures throughout Trump's campaign. The disconnect between her testimony and the documented failures created an credibility crisis that made her continued leadership impossible.

Cheatle stepped down on July 23, acknowledging that the Secret Service had failed in its fundamental mission to protect those under its care. Her resignation marked the beginning of a broader reckoning within the agency about resource allocation, threat assessment, and coordination protocols that had proven inadequate for the modern security environment. The director's departure also cleared the way for more comprehensive reforms and investigations that would have been difficult to pursue while she remained in position, though it left the agency in the difficult position of rebuilding its reputation while continuing to face ongoing threats.

Congressional Task Force Formation

The magnitude of the security failures revealed by the assassination attempt prompted Congress to establish a bipartisan Task Force on the Attempted Assassination of Donald J. Trump, representing the most comprehensive legislative investigation into protective service failures since the Warren Commission's examination of President Kennedy's murder. House Speaker Mike Johnson and Democratic Leader Hakeem Jeffries announced the task force formation on July 24, with the House voting unanimously to create the investigative body that would have broad subpoena powers and access to classified information.

The task force was structured to ensure bipartisan credibility, with Representatives Mike Kelly of Pennsylvania serving as chairman and Jason Crow of Colorado as ranking member. This leadership arrangement reflected Congress's recognition that the investigation needed to transcend partisan politics to restore public confidence in protective services. The task force's mandate extended beyond the immediate failures at Butler to examine broader questions about threat assessment, resource allocation, and coordination between federal and local law enforcement agencies.

Over the following months, the task force conducted 46 interviews with local, state, and federal officials involved in the Butler rally security arrangements, ultimately producing a comprehensive final report on December 10, 2024. The investigation revealed stunning communication failures, inadequate resource allocation, and systemic problems that went far beyond individual mistakes or isolated incidents. The task force's work provided the most authoritative account of what had gone wrong at Butler while offering recommendations for preventing similar failures in the future, though its findings would also become part of the ongoing political debate about responsibility and reform.

CHAPTER 9: THE DIVINE PROVIDENCE NARRATIVE

The bullet that grazed Donald Trump's ear on July 13, 2024, missed ending his life by approximately two inches—a margin so narrow that many of his supporters immediately interpreted his survival as evidence of divine intervention in American politics. Within hours of the assassination attempt, religious language began permeating discussions of Trump's survival, with evangelical leaders and ordinary believers alike describing the near-miss as a miracle that revealed God's plan for America. This wasn't merely political rhetoric or campaign messaging; it represented a genuine theological interpretation of current events that would fundamentally reshape how millions of Americans understood both Trump's candidacy and their own role in defending what they saw as a divinely ordained mission.

The religious narrative that emerged from Butler, Pennsylvania, tapped into deep currents of American civil religion and evangelical political theology that had been building throughout Trump's political career. His survival became proof not just of his personal resilience, but of divine protection for a leader chosen to restore Christian values to American governance. This providential interpretation of the assassination attempt would prove to be one of the most powerful elements of Trump's campaign, creating an emotional and spiritual connection with religious voters that transcended typical political loyalties and transformed electoral participation into an act of religious devotion.

Trump's Religious Interpretation

Donald Trump's own interpretation of his survival reflected both genuine belief and shrewd political instinct, as he recognized the profound impact that religious framing could have on his campaign's trajectory. In recent conversations with those close to the president, they revealed that July 13th made Trump believe that God had a hand in his 2024 victory, adding a spiritual dimension to his political comeback that had been largely absent from his previous campaigns. This wasn't merely campaign rhetoric but appeared to represent a genuine shift in how Trump understood his own destiny and political mission.

Trump began incorporating explicitly religious language into his campaign speeches, describing his survival as evidence that he had been spared for a divine purpose. He frequently referenced the narrowness of his escape—the two inches that separated life from death—as proof that supernatural forces were protecting him from enemies who sought to prevent his return to power. This religious interpretation allowed Trump to cast his political opponents not just as policy adversaries but as enemies of divine will, elevating the stakes of the election beyond normal democratic competition.

The former president's embrace of providential language also reflected his deep understanding of his evangelical base, who had long viewed him as an imperfect vessel chosen by God to advance Christian causes in American politics. His survival narrative provided theological validation for supporters who had sometimes struggled to reconcile Trump's personal conduct with their religious beliefs. The assassination attempt became evidence that God was indeed working through Trump, regardless of his human flaws, to accomplish divine purposes in American governance.

Evangelical Support Solidifies

The assassination attempt crystallized evangelical support for Trump in ways that years of traditional campaigning had not achieved, creating a sense of spiritual urgency around his candidacy that transcended normal political enthusiasm. Prominent evangelical leaders immediately interpreted Trump's survival as a sign of divine favor, with many drawing parallels to biblical accounts of God protecting chosen leaders from their enemies. This theological framework transformed electoral participation from civic duty into religious obligation, motivating evangelical voters to view supporting Trump as an act of faithfulness to divine will.

Several media personalities and Trump himself suggested his survival was a miracle and that the GOP nominee was spared by divine intervention. Poll data revealed the depth of this religious interpretation: 66% of registered Republicans surveyed said Trump was "favored by divine providence or God's will," while only 11% of Democrats agreed. This stark partisan divide in theological interpretation reflected how completely religious and political identities had merged within Trump's coalition, creating a voting bloc motivated by spiritual conviction rather than mere policy preferences.

Evangelical churches across America began incorporating Trump's survival into their prayer services and sermon illustrations, treating July 13th as a moment of divine intervention in American history. Many pastors described the assassination attempt as evidence that spiritual warfare was being fought through political means, with Trump serving as God's chosen instrument against forces seeking to destroy Christian civilization. This religious mobilization created unprecedented enthusiasm among evangelical voters, who saw the

58

election not as a choice between candidates but as a battle between good and evil with eternal consequences.

"God Saved Trump" Movement

The "God Saved Trump" movement emerged organically from grassroots religious communities rather than top-down campaign organizing, demonstrating the authentic spiritual interpretation that many Americans placed on the assassination attempt. Social media platforms filled with testimonials from believers who described watching the shooting and immediately recognizing divine intervention in Trump's survival. Prayer groups, Bible studies, and religious gatherings began incorporating Trump's survival into their regular worship, treating July 13th as a modern miracle worthy of celebration and thanksgiving.

Religious merchandise featuring images of Trump's bloodied but defiant pose combined with biblical verses about divine protection became bestsellers among evangelical consumers. T-shirts, bumper stickers, and artwork depicting Trump surrounded by angels or protected by divine light transformed the assassination attempt into religious iconography that reinforced the providential narrative. This commercialization of Trump's survival reflected genuine religious sentiment rather than mere political marketing, as believers sought tangible ways to express their theological interpretation of current events.

The movement also manifested in organized prayer campaigns specifically focused on Trump's protection and electoral success, with many evangelical groups treating his victory as essential to

God's plan for America. Churches organized special services thanking God for Trump's survival while praying for his continued protection and electoral triumph. These religious activities created powerful community bonds among Trump supporters, who shared not just political preferences but spiritual convictions about the cosmic significance of the 2024 election.

Faith and Politics Intertwined

The assassination attempt completed the transformation of Trump's political movement into something approaching a religious crusade, where support for his candidacy became inseparable from religious identity and spiritual conviction. This fusion of faith and politics created unprecedented intensity among religious voters, who understood their electoral participation as obedience to divine command rather than mere civic engagement. The line between political rally and religious revival became increasingly blurred as Trump's campaign events incorporated prayer, religious music, and explicitly theological language about America's spiritual destiny.

The religious interpretation of Trump's survival also provided theological justification for political actions that might otherwise seem extreme or un-Christian to traditional evangelical sensibilities. If God had miraculously saved Trump from assassination, then supporting him became a religious duty that superseded conventional political norms or moral considerations. This theological framework allowed religious voters to embrace increasingly militant political rhetoric while maintaining their spiritual self-image as faithful Christians following divine guidance.

The intertwining of faith and politics around Trump's survival narrative created a powerful but potentially dangerous precedent for American democratic life, where political opposition could be framed as opposition to God's will. This theological interpretation of partisan politics elevated normal democratic competition to the level of spiritual warfare, making compromise or peaceful coexistence with political opponents increasingly difficult to justify on religious grounds. The "God Saved Trump" movement demonstrated both the power of religious conviction in American politics and the risks of sanctifying partisan political positions with divine authority.

CHAPTER 10: MILWAUKEE TRIUMPH

The Republican National Convention in Milwaukee, Wisconsin, was supposed to be a celebration of Trump's inevitable nomination and a launching pad for the general election campaign. Instead, it became something far more dramatic and historically significant—the triumphant return of an assassination survivor to claim his party's nomination while the nation watched in fascination and awe. When Trump walked onto the convention stage on July 15, just two days after the Butler shooting, wearing a white bandage over his wounded right ear, he transformed what could have been a moment of vulnerability into perhaps the most powerful political theater in modern American history.

The convention hall erupted in sustained applause, tears, and chants as delegates and observers witnessed something unprecedented: a presidential candidate whose survival had literally been measured in inches taking the stage to accept his party's nomination. The bandaged ear became an instant symbol of Trump's sacrifice and resilience, while his presence served as living proof that American democracy could not be silenced by an assassin's bullet. The Milwaukee convention would be remembered not just as Trump's nomination ceremony, but as the moment when his survival narrative was crystallized into a political movement that would carry him back to the White House.

The Bandaged Ear Entrance

Trump's entrance at the Republican National Convention created one of the most emotionally charged moments in modern political history, as delegates rose to their feet in sustained applause that lasted several minutes. The white bandage covering his wounded right ear served as a visible reminder of how close America had come to losing a former president to political violence, transforming what could have been a routine nomination acceptance into something approaching a resurrection appearance. Many delegates were visibly emotional, with tears streaming down faces as they witnessed Trump's defiant survival in person.

The bandage itself became an iconic symbol that transcended typical political imagery, representing not just Trump's personal resilience but the idea that American democracy itself had survived an existential attack. Unlike typical political props or staged symbols, the bandage was authentic evidence of real violence and genuine survival, providing credibility that no amount of campaign staging could manufacture. The visual contrast between the clinical white bandage and Trump's otherwise polished appearance created a powerful juxtaposition that reinforced his narrative as a leader who had literally bled for his cause.

Trump's decision to appear publicly with the bandage rather than attempting to conceal his injury demonstrated the political instincts that had defined his career—transforming potential weakness into displays of strength. The bandage became a badge of honor that validated every claim Trump had made about facing persecution and surviving attacks from enemies who sought to destroy him. His willingness to display his wound publicly sent a message to supporters that he was unashamed of his survival and determined to continue fighting despite the danger.

JD Vance Selection

The announcement of JD Vance as Trump's vice presidential running mate came less than 48 hours after the assassination attempt, creating an unusual dynamic where the VP selection was overshadowed by the dramatic events in Butler yet also benefited from the increased attention and sympathy generated by Trump's survival. Vance, the author of "Hillbilly Elegy" and Ohio Senator, represented Trump's attempt to solidify support among working-class white voters while appealing to younger conservatives who could help expand his coalition beyond his traditional base.

The timing of Vance's selection amid the assassination attempt created instant credibility for the ticket's narrative about facing persecution from establishment forces. Vance had been a vocal critic of what he saw as elite contempt for ordinary Americans, making him a natural choice to amplify Trump's message about surviving attacks from enemies who despised traditional American values. His selection reinforced the theme that Trump's ticket represented authentic Americans fighting against corrupt institutions that would resort to violence to maintain power.

Vance's acceptance speech at the convention took on added significance as he spoke directly about the assassination attempt and what it revealed about the stakes of the election. His youth and rhetorical skills complemented Trump's survival narrative while providing the ticket with someone who could articulate the broader implications of July 13th for American democracy. The VP selection became part of the larger story about Trump's miraculous survival and determination to continue fighting for forgotten Americans despite mortal danger.

Unity Message vs. Fight Message

The Republican National Convention created tension between two competing narratives that Trump's team struggled to balance throughout the four-day event. The assassination attempt had generated calls from across the political spectrum for lowering the temperature of American political rhetoric, creating pressure for Trump to deliver a unifying message that could heal national divisions and prevent future violence. Many advisers urged Trump to use his survival as an opportunity to position himself as a healer who could bring Americans together after a moment of national trauma.

However, Trump's political instincts and the energy of his base pulled him toward the more combative "Fight! Fight! Fight!" message that had emerged from the assassination attempt itself. His supporters hadn't come to Milwaukee to hear calls for unity with the same political forces they believed had created the atmosphere that led to the shooting—they wanted validation that their movement would continue fighting against enemies who had literally tried to kill their leader. The tension between these competing messages played out throughout the convention as Trump oscillated between calls for national healing and defiant promises to defeat his opponents.

Ultimately, Trump chose to emphasize the fight message while paying lip service to unity themes, recognizing that his base was energized by survival rather than reconciliation. The convention became a celebration of Trump's defiance rather than a call for political peace, with speakers repeatedly referencing the assassination attempt as evidence that the stakes of the election were literally life and death. This choice to prioritize confrontation over conciliation would define the remainder of Trump's campaign and set the tone for how he would interpret his electoral mandate.

Convention Bounce

The Republican National Convention generated what political analysts immediately recognized as one of the most significant polling bounces in modern presidential campaign history, though the assassination attempt made it difficult to separate the convention's impact from the survival narrative's effect on voter sentiment. Traditional convention bounces typically last only a few weeks and provide modest improvements in polling numbers, but Trump's Milwaukee appearance created sustained enthusiasm that carried through the remainder of the campaign season.

Polling data showed Trump gaining ground in key swing states immediately following the convention, with particular strength among voters who cited his survival and resilience as factors in their support. The convention's emotional impact extended beyond typical Republican voters to include independents and even some Democrats who were impressed by Trump's response to the assassination attempt. Focus groups revealed that many viewers saw Trump's bandaged ear appearance as evidence of authentic leadership under pressure, creating credibility that traditional campaign messaging could not achieve.

The convention bounce was amplified by media coverage that focused heavily on the dramatic nature of Trump's survival story and his defiant return to the political stage. Cable news networks provided extensive coverage of emotional moments from the convention floor, while social media platforms filled with user-generated content celebrating Trump's resilience. The sustained media attention meant that the convention's impact extended far beyond the typical four-day news cycle, creating momentum that would carry Trump through the crucial summer months when many voters begin paying closer attention to presidential campaigns.

CHAPTER 11: THE SEPTEMBER ATTEMPT

Just sixty-four days after Thomas Matthew Crooks's rifle fire shattered the summer evening in Butler, Pennsylvania, Donald Trump found himself once again in the crosshairs of a would-be assassin. On September 15, 2024, while enjoying what should have been a routine round of golf at his Trump International Golf Club in West Palm Beach, Florida, the former president came within yards of another gunman who had been lying in wait for nearly twelve hours. This second assassination attempt differed dramatically from the chaos and heroics of Butler—there were no dramatic photographs, no defiant fist-pumping, and no inspiring imagery of survival against impossible odds.

Instead, the Florida incident revealed a more troubling reality: that the assassination attempt in Pennsylvania had not been an isolated moment of political violence but rather the beginning of a pattern that would define the remainder of the 2024 campaign. The fact that two separate individuals, with no apparent connection to each other, had attempted to kill Trump within just over two months suggested that the political climate had reached a level of toxicity where violence against candidates had become almost inevitable. Yet paradoxically, this second brush with death would have far less political impact than the first, demonstrating how quickly even assassination attempts could become normalized in the fractured landscape of American politics.

Ryan Wesley Routh at Trump International

Ryan Wesley Routh presented a very different profile from Thomas Matthew Crooks, the young man who had carried out the Butler assassination attempt. At 58 years old, Routh was a small construction company owner from Hawaii whose path to attempted political murder revealed the complex and often contradictory motivations that could drive individuals toward violence. Unlike Crooks, whose political leanings remained largely mysterious, Routh had a documented history of political engagement that included both supporting and opposing Trump at different times, reflecting the kind of unstable political identity that characterized many Americans during the polarized 2024 election cycle.

Routh had spent considerable time in Ukraine supporting the war effort against Russia, even attempting to recruit foreign fighters for the Ukrainian cause through social media posts and interviews with international media. His obsession with the conflict had apparently evolved into a broader hostility toward Trump, whom he viewed as insufficiently supportive of Ukraine's struggle for independence. In a letter written months before his arrest, Routh stated: "this was an assassination attempt on Donald Trump but I am so sorry I failed you. I tried my best and gave it all the gumption I could muster."

The would-be assassin had been planning his attack for months, demonstrating a level of premeditation that distinguished his attempt from Crooks's apparently more spontaneous decision to target the Butler rally. Routh had positioned himself in the bushes surrounding Trump's golf course for approximately twelve hours before being spotted by a Secret Service agent, showing remarkable patience and commitment to his deadly mission. His careful planning and extended surveillance suggested a more sophisticated approach to

69

assassination than the relatively impulsive attack that had occurred in Pennsylvania.

A Very Different Kind of Threat

The September attempt revealed how the security challenges facing presidential candidates had evolved beyond the traditional models of protection that the Secret Service had developed over decades. Unlike the Butler shooting, which occurred at a public rally with thousands of attendees, the golf course incident involved a private venue where Trump's presence was supposed to be unpredictable and secure. The fact that Routh could position himself for hours within striking distance of a former president demonstrated how modern technology and patient surveillance could circumvent even enhanced security measures.

Law enforcement officials noted that the golf course's perimeter was not fully secured because Trump was not an incumbent president, reflecting the resource constraints and policy decisions that continued to leave candidates vulnerable despite the lessons of Butler. The Secret Service did not search the perimeter of the golf course because Trump's visit there was not a scheduled event, treating it as a spontaneous personal activity rather than a security risk requiring comprehensive protection. This approach proved dangerously inadequate when facing a determined assassin willing to wait for opportunities.

The attack method itself—lying in wait with a rifle near a location Trump was known to frequent—represented a more patient and methodical approach to assassination than the direct assault attempted at Butler. Routh's positioning in dense vegetation provided concealment while maintaining sight lines to the golf course, demonstrating how relatively simple tactics could create significant security vulnerabilities. The incident forced a fundamental reevaluation of how to protect political figures during private activities that had previously been considered low-risk situations.

Diminished Public Impact

Despite being the second assassination attempt against Trump within just over two months, the Florida incident generated significantly less public attention and political impact than the Butler shooting. The absence of dramatic visuals played a crucial role in this diminished response—where Butler had produced iconic imagery of Trump's bloodied but defiant survival, the golf course attempt offered only mundane details about a suspect fleeing through bushes after being spotted by alert security personnel. News anchors reported that Trump had been playing golf when the potential shooter was detected, lacking the heroic narrative that had emerged from Pennsylvania.

The timing of the attempt also contributed to its reduced political impact, occurring just as the general election campaign was intensifying and voters were becoming focused on more traditional political issues like the economy and policy differences between candidates. The novelty of assassination attempts had worn off to some degree, with the public having already processed the implications of political violence during the extensive coverage of the Butler incident. This normalization of threats against political figures represented a troubling development in American political culture.

Public polling showed that while Americans remained concerned about political violence, the second attempt did not generate the same emotional response or sympathy for Trump that had followed the Butler shooting. The lack of actual gunfire and Trump's safe evacuation meant that the incident felt more like a security scare than a genuine brush with death, reducing its psychological impact on voters who had already incorporated the reality of assassination threats into their understanding of the election. The diminished response revealed how quickly even extraordinary events could become routine in the accelerated news cycle of modern politics.

Security Enhancements

The September assassination attempt prompted immediate and comprehensive changes to Trump's security arrangements that transformed how the Secret Service approached protection for the remainder of the campaign. The golf course incident demonstrated that traditional security models based on securing public events were inadequate for protecting candidates during private activities at venues they frequented regularly. Secret Service protocols were expanded to include comprehensive perimeter security for all locations where Trump might spend extended time, regardless of whether visits were officially scheduled or considered private.

The most visible change was the installation of bulletproof glass barriers at all outdoor Trump campaign events, creating a protective envelope that had previously been reserved for sitting presidents. These barriers became a permanent fixture at Trump rallies, changing the visual dynamic of his events while providing tangible evidence of the ongoing security threats he faced. The glass barriers served both practical and symbolic purposes, protecting Trump while reminding audiences of his survival and the dangers he continued to face.

Advanced surveillance technology was deployed around Trump's regular locations, including drone detection systems and expanded human surveillance networks designed to identify potential threats before they could position themselves for attacks. The Secret Service also enhanced coordination with local law enforcement agencies, addressing the communication failures that had contributed to the Butler shooting's near success. These security enhancements represented the most significant expansion of candidate protection in decades, fundamentally altering how presidential campaigns would be conducted in the future while acknowledging that the threat environment had permanently changed.

CHAPTER 12: BULLETPROOF GLASS AND BIGGER CROWDS

The most visible legacy of July 13th was not found in polling data or political analysis, but in the sheets of bulletproof glass that now surrounded Donald Trump at every outdoor campaign event. The transparent barriers, reaching eight feet high and extending in a protective semicircle around the candidate's podium, served as constant reminders that the 2024 election was being conducted under the shadow of attempted assassination. What had once been intimate encounters between candidate and crowd now resembled presidential-level security, with Trump speaking from behind protective barriers that both safeguarded his life and symbolized the extraordinary circumstances of his comeback campaign.

Yet paradoxically, these enhanced security measures coincided with the largest crowds of Trump's entire political career, as Americans flocked to witness the candidate who had survived an assassin's bullet and returned to fight for the presidency. The assassination attempt had transformed Trump from a controversial political figure into something approaching a folk hero, drawing supporters who wanted to demonstrate their solidarity with a leader who had literally bled for his cause. The bulletproof glass became a powerful visual metaphor for Trump's entire campaign—a candidate under siege but unbroken, protected but not silenced, speaking truth to power from behind barriers that enemies had forced him to erect.

Enhanced Security Measures

The security transformations following the assassination attempts created the most comprehensive candidate protection system in

American political history, fundamentally altering how presidential campaigns would be conducted for generations to come. Bulletproof glass barriers became standard at all outdoor Trump events, creating a protective envelope that had previously been reserved for sitting presidents but was now extended to a candidate whose life had been threatened multiple times. These barriers, while transparent, created a psychological and physical barrier between Trump and his audience that changed the intimate dynamics that had defined his rallies since 2015.

Advanced surveillance technology was deployed at every Trump event, including counter-sniper teams positioned on surrounding buildings, drone detection systems designed to identify aerial threats, and expanded security perimeters that pushed potential attackers much further from the candidate. The Secret Service coordinate with local law enforcement agencies was enhanced dramatically, addressing the communication failures that had contributed to the Butler shooting's near success. These improvements required significantly more resources and personnel than traditional candidate protection, reflecting the permanent elevation in threat level that Trump now faced.

The security enhancements extended beyond public events to include comprehensive protection at Trump's private residences, golf courses, and other regular destinations where he might be vulnerable to patient attackers like Ryan Wesley Routh. Advanced perimeter monitoring, regular security sweeps, and continuous surveillance created a protective bubble around Trump that resembled presidential-level security while he remained a candidate. These measures represented an unprecedented expansion of Secret Service resources and demonstrated the agency's determination to prevent additional assassination attempts through overwhelming security presence.

Rally Attendance Surges

The assassination attempt created an unexpected surge in rally attendance as Americans across the country sought to witness firsthand the candidate who had survived an assassin's bullet and returned to the campaign trail. Trump's events began drawing crowds that exceeded even his legendary 2016 rallies, with attendance figures reaching record levels as supporters traveled hundreds of miles to demonstrate their solidarity with a leader they viewed as having been martyred for their cause. The assassination attempt had transformed routine campaign events into historical moments that Americans wanted to witness personally.

The crowds that gathered at post-Butler rallies displayed a different energy and emotional intensity than typical political events, with many attendees describing their attendance as both political statement and pilgrimage to honor Trump's survival. Focus groups revealed that significant numbers of rallygoers had never attended political events before but felt compelled to show support for a candidate who had risked his life for his beliefs. The assassination attempt had created a sense of urgency and historical significance that motivated previously inactive Americans to participate actively in the democratic process.

The surge in attendance created logistical challenges as venues that had been adequate for pre-assassination crowds proved insufficient for the numbers seeking to attend Trump's events. Campaign

76

organizers had to seek larger venues and implement more sophisticated crowd management systems to accommodate the increased demand while maintaining the security protocols necessitated by ongoing threats. The larger crowds also generated more extensive media coverage, creating a positive feedback loop that amplified the impact of Trump's survival narrative throughout the remainder of the campaign.

The Martyrdom Factor

The assassination attempt created a powerful martyrdom narrative that fundamentally altered how Trump's supporters viewed his candidacy and their own role in defending democracy. The blood that had streamed down Trump's face at Butler became tangible evidence that he had literally shed blood for his political beliefs, creating a level of emotional connection and personal loyalty that transcended typical candidate-voter relationships. Supporters began describing Trump in explicitly sacrificial terms, viewing his willingness to continue campaigning despite mortal danger as evidence of selfless devotion to American values.

This martyrdom narrative was reinforced by Trump's decision to continue holding large public rallies despite the obvious security risks, demonstrating what supporters interpreted as courage in the face of ongoing threats. Each subsequent rally became both a political event and an act of defiance against forces that had tried to silence him through violence. The bulletproof glass barriers served as visual reminders of the price Trump was willing to pay for his political convictions, creating sympathy and admiration that extended beyond his traditional base of support.

The martyrdom factor also provided Trump with moral authority that proved difficult for opponents to challenge, as criticism of someone who had survived an assassination attempt could be portrayed as callous or unpatriotic. The assassination attempt created a protective political narrative that insulated Trump from typical campaign attacks while positioning him as a victim of forces seeking to subvert democratic processes. This martyrdom narrative became central to Trump's appeal during the final months of the campaign, motivating supporters who saw defending him as defending democracy itself.

Campaign Strategy Shifts

The assassination attempt forced Trump's campaign to fundamentally reconsider its strategic approach, balancing the political advantages of the survival narrative against the practical constraints imposed by enhanced security requirements. Campaign events became more carefully orchestrated productions designed to maximize the visual impact of Trump speaking from behind bulletproof glass while maintaining the energy and spontaneity that had defined his political brand. The security measures created new opportunities for dramatic staging that emphasized Trump's continued vulnerability while celebrating his refusal to be intimidated.

Campaign messaging evolved to place Trump's survival at the center of broader themes about perseverance, strength, and divine providence that resonated with voters seeking leadership during uncertain times. The assassination attempt provided credible evidence for claims about the stakes of the election and the lengths to which opponents would go to prevent Trump's return to power. This martyrdom narrative became integrated into virtually every aspect of the campaign's communication strategy, from fundraising appeals to policy discussions to voter mobilization efforts.

The campaign also recognized that Trump's survival story had unique power to reach voters who might be skeptical of traditional political messaging but could appreciate authentic displays of courage under fire. Focus groups revealed that the assassination attempt had created credibility for Trump among demographics that had previously viewed him negatively, as his response to genuine crisis provided evidence of character that campaign advertisements could never manufacture. The strategic shift toward emphasizing survival and resilience over policy details reflected the campaign's understanding that emotional connection often matters more than rational argument in motivating voter behavior.

CHAPTER 13: BIDEN'S EXIT AND HARRIS'S RISE

Just eight days after Donald Trump's triumphant appearance at the Republican National Convention with his bandaged ear, the 2024 presidential race was turned upside down by an announcement that few saw coming. On July 21, 2024, President Joe Biden published a letter on social media announcing his withdrawal from the presidential race and endorsing Vice President Kamala Harris as his successor. The decision, which came after weeks of mounting pressure from Democratic leaders concerned about Biden's debate performance and age-related questions, fundamentally altered the dynamics of an election that had seemed to be moving inexorably in Trump's favor following his survival of the assassination attempt.

Biden's exit created an immediate political earthquake that shifted media attention away from Trump's survival narrative and toward the historic nature of Harris's candidacy as the first Black woman to lead a major party's presidential ticket. The assassination attempt, which had dominated headlines for over a week and seemed destined to define the remainder of the campaign, suddenly became part of a larger story about dramatic political upheaval and changing electoral dynamics. President Biden's decision to drop out of the 2024 race and endorse Vice President Harris upended the presidential race and drastically shifted the media coverage toward the Democrats, creating new challenges for Trump's campaign just as they had seemed to establish decisive momentum.

July 21st - Biden Steps Down

President Biden's decision to withdraw from the 2024 presidential race represented one of the most dramatic political reversals in modern American history, as the incumbent president abandoned his reelection campaign at the moment when such decisions typically become irreversible. The announcement came via a carefully crafted letter posted to social media, in which Biden cited his desire to focus on his presidential duties while passing the torch to a new generation of Democratic leadership. The timing, just days after Trump's convention triumph and amid ongoing discussions about the assassination attempt's political impact, suggested that Democratic leaders had concluded their chances were better with a different candidate despite the challenges of such a late change.

The decision followed weeks of intense private pressure from Democratic congressional leaders, major donors, and party officials who had grown increasingly concerned about Biden's ability to defeat Trump following his disastrous June 27 debate performance. Less than a week after the shooting, more Democratic leaders had resumed calling on Biden to resign, and Democratic members of Congress had rebuffed a proposal to nominate Biden before the August Democratic National Convention. The assassination attempt had provided temporary respite from calls for Biden to step aside, but the underlying concerns about his candidacy remained unresolved.

Biden's withdrawal letter emphasized his accomplishments as president while acknowledging that stepping aside was in the best interests of both the Democratic Party and the country. The decision required extraordinary political courage, as sitting presidents virtually never abandon reelection campaigns voluntarily. Biden's choice to prioritize party success over personal ambition would be remembered as either an act of selfless statesmanship or a devastating admission that Democrats lacked confidence in their ability to defeat Trump even after he had survived an assassination attempt.

Kamala Harris Takes the Stage

Kamala Harris's ascension to the top of the Democratic ticket created immediate excitement within the party while presenting significant challenges in organizing a presidential campaign with just over three months remaining before Election Day. Harris had the advantage of inheriting Biden's campaign infrastructure, fundraising network, and delegate commitments, but she also carried the burden of defending the administration's record while differentiating herself sufficiently to generate enthusiasm among voters who had been lukewarm about Biden's candidacy. Her selection represented a historic breakthrough as the first Black woman and first person of South Asian descent to lead a major party's presidential ticket.

The vice president moved quickly to consolidate Democratic support, receiving endorsements from major party leaders, labor unions, and progressive organizations within hours of Biden's announcement. Her campaign raised over $100 million in the first 24 hours after her candidacy was announced, demonstrating the pent-up enthusiasm among Democratic donors who had been concerned about Biden's prospects. Harris's fundraising success provided immediate evidence that her candidacy could energize Democratic voters in ways that Biden's reelection campaign had struggled to achieve.

Harris also benefited from what many Democratic strategists privately acknowledged was favorable timing, as her entrance into the race coincided with peak media attention on Trump's assassination attempt and convention activities. Her historic candidacy provided a compelling counter-narrative to Trump's survival story, shifting media focus toward questions about breaking barriers and generational change rather than Trump's resilience and divine protection. The juxtaposition between Trump's martyrdom narrative and Harris's barrier-breaking candidacy created competing storylines that complicated the political environment for both campaigns.

Momentum Shifts

Harris's entry into the presidential race created an immediate shift in campaign momentum that caught Trump's team off guard after weeks of believing they had established decisive advantages following the assassination attempt. Polling data began showing movement toward Democrats within days of Harris's announcement, as voters who had been reluctant to support Biden's reelection expressed new enthusiasm for Harris's candidacy. The change was particularly pronounced among younger voters, Black voters, and college-educated suburbanites who represented crucial demographic groups that Democrats needed to mobilize for victory.

Media coverage shifted dramatically from focus on Trump's survival and Republican convention success toward analysis of Harris's historic candidacy and the challenges facing both campaigns in the abbreviated general election timeline. The assassination attempt, which had seemed likely to dominate political discourse through Election Day, was suddenly competing for attention with coverage of Harris's campaign launch, running mate selection process, and

83

policy positions. This media shift denied Trump's campaign the sustained coverage of his survival narrative that they had expected to leverage throughout the remainder of the campaign.

The momentum shift was also reflected in grassroots political activity, as Democratic volunteer sign-ups surged and Harris campaign events began drawing the kind of large, enthusiastic crowds that had been absent from Biden's reelection effort. Focus groups revealed that many Democrats who had been resigned to supporting Biden out of duty were genuinely excited about Harris's candidacy, creating energy that translated into increased fundraising, volunteer activity, and voter registration efforts. The enthusiasm gap that had favored Republicans following the assassination attempt began to narrow as Democrats found new reasons for optimism about their electoral prospects.

Polls Tighten

The immediate polling impact of Harris's candidacy was dramatic, with survey data showing significant movement toward Democrats that eliminated much of the advantage Trump had gained following the assassination attempt and Republican convention. National polls that had shown Trump leading Biden by several points began showing a competitive race, with some surveys indicating Harris had erased Trump's lead entirely within weeks of entering the race. On July 1, an aggregate of national general election polls showed Trump had a three-point lead over Harris (43.8% to 40.8%), but by August 17, these polls showed Harris ahead of Trump by more than two points (46.7% to 44.4%), representing a five-point swing in less than two months.

Battleground state polling showed even more dramatic shifts, particularly in the Rust Belt states that both campaigns understood would likely determine the election outcome. In Michigan, Pennsylvania, and Wisconsin, surveys that had shown Biden tied or slightly behind Trump began showing Harris with small but consistent leads. A New York Times/Siena College poll from August 5-9 showed Harris leading Trump by four points in these three crucial states (50% to 46%), representing a significant improvement from Biden's position in the same states just months earlier.

The polling shifts forced Trump's campaign to reconsider their strategic approach, as the post-assassination bump that had seemed to provide decisive advantages was being eroded by Harris's candidacy and the Democratic Party's renewed energy. Internal Republican polling showed similar trends, with Trump advisers acknowledging privately that Harris presented a more formidable opponent than Biden would have been. The tightening polls also affected media coverage and donor confidence, as the race returned to the competitive dynamics that had characterized most presidential elections rather than the potential landslide that some had predicted following Trump's survival and Biden's struggles.

CHAPTER 14: THE ASSASSINATION ATTEMPTS AS CAMPAIGN TOOLS

Just eight days after Donald Trump's triumphant appearance at the Republican National Convention with his bandaged ear, the 2024 presidential race was turned upside down by an announcement that few saw coming. On July 21, 2024, President Joe Biden published a letter on social media announcing his withdrawal from the presidential race and endorsing Vice President Kamala Harris as his successor. The decision, which came after weeks of mounting pressure from Democratic leaders concerned about Biden's debate performance and age-related questions, fundamentally altered the dynamics of an election that had seemed to be moving inexorably in Trump's favor following his survival of the assassination attempt.

Biden's exit created an immediate political earthquake that shifted media attention away from Trump's survival narrative and toward the historic nature of Harris's candidacy as the first Black woman to lead a major party's presidential ticket. The assassination attempt, which had dominated headlines for over a week and seemed destined to define the remainder of the campaign, suddenly became part of a larger story about dramatic political upheaval and changing electoral dynamics. President Biden's decision to drop out of the 2024 race and endorse Vice President Harris upended the presidential race and drastically shifted the media coverage toward the Democrats, creating new challenges for Trump's campaign just as they had seemed to establish decisive momentum.

July 21st - Biden Steps Down

President Biden's decision to withdraw from the 2024 presidential race represented one of the most dramatic political reversals in modern American history, as the incumbent president abandoned his reelection campaign at the moment when such decisions typically become irreversible. The announcement came via a carefully crafted letter posted to social media, in which Biden cited his desire to focus on his presidential duties while passing the torch to a new generation of Democratic leadership. The timing, just days after Trump's convention triumph and amid ongoing discussions about the assassination attempt's political impact, suggested that Democratic leaders had concluded their chances were better with a different candidate despite the challenges of such a late change.

The decision followed weeks of intense private pressure from Democratic congressional leaders, major donors, and party officials who had grown increasingly concerned about Biden's ability to defeat Trump following his disastrous June 27 debate performance. Less than a week after the shooting, more Democratic leaders had resumed calling on Biden to resign, and Democratic members of Congress had rebuffed a proposal to nominate Biden before the August Democratic National Convention. The assassination attempt had provided temporary respite from calls for Biden to step aside, but the underlying concerns about his candidacy remained unresolved.

Biden's withdrawal letter emphasized his accomplishments as president while acknowledging that stepping aside was in the best interests of both the Democratic Party and the country. The decision required extraordinary political courage, as sitting presidents virtually never abandon reelection campaigns voluntarily. Biden's

87

choice to prioritize party success over personal ambition would be remembered as either an act of selfless statesmanship or a devastating admission that Democrats lacked confidence in their ability to defeat Trump even after he had survived an assassination attempt.

Kamala Harris Takes the Stage

Kamala Harris's ascension to the top of the Democratic ticket created immediate excitement within the party while presenting significant challenges in organizing a presidential campaign with just over three months remaining before Election Day. Harris had the advantage of inheriting Biden's campaign infrastructure, fundraising network, and delegate commitments, but she also carried the burden of defending the administration's record while differentiating herself sufficiently to generate enthusiasm among voters who had been lukewarm about Biden's candidacy. Her selection represented a historic breakthrough as the first Black woman and first person of South Asian descent to lead a major party's presidential ticket.

The vice president moved quickly to consolidate Democratic support, receiving endorsements from major party leaders, labor unions, and progressive organizations within hours of Biden's announcement. Her campaign raised over $100 million in the first 24 hours after her candidacy was announced, demonstrating the pent-up enthusiasm among Democratic donors who had been concerned about Biden's prospects. Harris's fundraising success provided immediate evidence that her candidacy could energize Democratic voters in ways that Biden's reelection campaign had struggled to achieve.

Harris also benefited from what many Democratic strategists privately acknowledged was favorable timing, as her entrance into the race coincided with peak media attention on Trump's assassination attempt and convention activities. Her historic candidacy provided a compelling counter-narrative to Trump's survival story, shifting media focus toward questions about breaking barriers and generational change rather than Trump's resilience and divine protection. The juxtaposition between Trump's martyrdom narrative and Harris's barrier-breaking candidacy created competing storylines that complicated the political environment for both campaigns.

Momentum Shifts

Harris's entry into the presidential race created an immediate shift in campaign momentum that caught Trump's team off guard after weeks of believing they had established decisive advantages following the assassination attempt. Polling data began showing movement toward Democrats within days of Harris's announcement, as voters who had been reluctant to support Biden's reelection expressed new enthusiasm for Harris's candidacy. The change was particularly pronounced among younger voters, Black voters, and college-educated suburbanites who represented crucial demographic groups that Democrats needed to mobilize for victory.

Media coverage shifted dramatically from focus on Trump's survival and Republican convention success toward analysis of Harris's historic candidacy and the challenges facing both campaigns in the abbreviated general election timeline. The assassination attempt, which had seemed likely to dominate political discourse through Election Day, was suddenly competing for attention with coverage of Harris's campaign launch, running mate selection process, and policy positions. This media shift denied Trump's campaign the sustained coverage of his survival narrative that they had expected to leverage throughout the remainder of the campaign.

The momentum shift was also reflected in grassroots political activity, as Democratic volunteer sign-ups surged and Harris campaign events began drawing the kind of large, enthusiastic crowds that had been absent from Biden's reelection effort. Focus groups revealed that many Democrats who had been resigned to supporting Biden out of duty were genuinely excited about Harris's candidacy, creating energy that translated into increased fundraising, volunteer activity, and voter registration efforts. The enthusiasm gap that had favored Republicans following the assassination attempt began to narrow as Democrats found new reasons for optimism about their electoral prospects.

Polls Tighten

The immediate polling impact of Harris's candidacy was dramatic, with survey data showing significant movement toward Democrats that eliminated much of the advantage Trump had gained following the assassination attempt and Republican convention. National polls that had shown Trump leading Biden by several points began showing a competitive race, with some surveys indicating Harris had erased Trump's lead entirely within weeks of entering the race. On July 1, an aggregate of national general election polls showed Trump had a three-point lead over Harris (43.8% to 40.8%), but by August 17, these polls showed Harris ahead of Trump by more than two points (46.7% to 44.4%), representing a five-point swing in less than two months.

Battleground state polling showed even more dramatic shifts, particularly in the Rust Belt states that both campaigns understood would likely determine the election outcome. In Michigan, Pennsylvania, and Wisconsin, surveys that had shown Biden tied or slightly behind Trump began showing Harris with small but consistent leads. A New York Times/Siena College poll from August 5-9 showed Harris leading Trump by four points in these three crucial states (50% to 46%), representing a significant improvement from Biden's position in the same states just months earlier.

The polling shifts forced Trump's campaign to reconsider their strategic approach, as the post-assassination bump that had seemed to provide decisive advantages was being eroded by Harris's candidacy and the Democratic Party's renewed energy. Internal Republican polling showed similar trends, with Trump advisers acknowledging privately that Harris presented a more formidable opponent than Biden would have been. The tightening polls also affected media coverage and donor confidence, as the race returned to the competitive dynamics that had characterized most presidential elections rather than the potential landslide that some had predicted following Trump's survival and Biden's struggles.

CHAPTER 15: OCTOBER SURPRISES

As the 2024 presidential campaign entered its final month, the traditional concept of "October surprises" seemed almost quaint compared to the extraordinary events that had already shaped the race. The assassination attempts, Biden's withdrawal, Harris's meteoric rise, and Trump's survival narrative had created such a dramatically altered political landscape that observers wondered what additional developments could possibly match the significance of what had already occurred. Yet October 2024 would prove that even in a campaign defined by unprecedented events, the final weeks could still produce moments that would influence the outcome of the most consequential election in modern American history.

The month brought a complex mixture of continued security threats, evolving voter sentiment, and polling data that suggested the race remained far closer than Trump's survival narrative might have predicted. Despite the powerful emotional appeal of his assassination survival and the religious interpretation many voters placed on his divine protection, Harris had successfully created a competitive race that defied early predictions of a Trump landslide. The final weeks would test whether Trump's martyrdom narrative could overcome traditional political dynamics around issues like the economy, abortion rights, and concerns about democratic institutions that continued to motivate significant portions of the American electorate.

Late Campaign Developments

The final month of the 2024 campaign featured a series of developments that demonstrated how Trump's survival narrative, while powerful, competed with other significant political storylines for voter attention. On October 12, 2024, a man was arrested near a checkpoint at a Trump rally in Coachella, California, possessing two firearms, ammunition, multiple passports with different names, and an unregistered vehicle with a fake license plate. While the incident was quickly contained and the individual's motivations remained unclear, it served as another reminder of the ongoing security threats that had become a constant feature of Trump's campaign events.

The Harris campaign worked systematically to shift focus away from Trump's survival story toward policy issues where they believed they held advantages, particularly abortion rights, healthcare, and concerns about Trump's rhetoric regarding democratic institutions. Harris's team recognized that while they couldn't compete with the emotional power of Trump's assassination survival, they could potentially motivate different voter segments through sustained focus on issues that had driven Democratic victories in previous elections. Late-breaking endorsements from prominent Republicans who cited concerns about Trump's fitness for office provided Harris with opportunities to appeal to moderate voters who might admire Trump's courage while remaining concerned about his leadership style.

International events also began influencing the campaign's final weeks, as conflicts in Eastern Europe and the Middle East created opportunities for both candidates to demonstrate their foreign policy credentials. Trump's survival narrative provided him with credibility on issues related to strength and resolve, while Harris attempted to position herself as offering more stable and predictable international leadership. The interplay between domestic political drama and international challenges created a complex environment where voters had to weigh Trump's personal resilience against broader concerns about American leadership on the global stage.

Security Scares Continue

The frequency of security incidents involving Trump throughout October demonstrated that the assassination attempts in July and September had not deterred other potential attackers but rather seemed to inspire additional threats against his life. Law enforcement agencies reported a significant increase in credible threats against Trump, requiring enhanced protective measures that went far beyond the bulletproof glass barriers that had become standard at his rallies. The Secret Service was forced to treat virtually every Trump appearance as a potential target for violence, creating security arrangements that resembled wartime protection for a political candidate.

Each new security scare reinforced Trump's narrative about facing unprecedented persecution while also raising questions about the sustainability of such intensive protection measures throughout a general election campaign. The Coachella incident, while successfully prevented, highlighted how potential attackers continued to view Trump's public appearances as opportunities for violence despite the obvious security enhancements that followed the earlier assassination attempts. These ongoing threats created a siege mentality among Trump's supporters while generating sympathy among voters who viewed the frequency of security incidents as evidence of the political establishment's hostility toward their candidate.

The psychological impact of constant security threats extended beyond Trump himself to affect his supporters, campaign staff, and even rally attendees who understood they were participating in events that had become magnets for potential violence. This atmosphere of danger paradoxically seemed to strengthen rather than weaken Trump's support among his base, as many supporters interpreted their willingness to attend potentially dangerous events as acts of courage and solidarity. The normalization of security threats as routine elements of Trump's campaign created an unprecedented dynamic where attending political rallies required conscious acceptance of personal risk in support of democratic participation.

Voter Sentiment Analysis

Comprehensive polling and focus group research conducted throughout October revealed complex and sometimes contradictory voter responses to Trump's survival narrative and its interaction with other campaign themes. While Trump's assassination survival had created genuine admiration for his personal courage across partisan lines, this respect didn't automatically translate into electoral support among voters who remained concerned about his policies, temperament, or impact on democratic institutions. Many voters expressed the ability to simultaneously respect Trump's bravery while preferring Harris's candidacy based on other considerations.

The martyrdom narrative that had energized Trump's religious base throughout the campaign showed signs of diminishing returns among secular voters who had initially been impressed by his survival but gradually returned their focus to traditional political concerns like economic policy and healthcare. Focus groups revealed that while the assassination attempts had created lasting

95

positive impressions of Trump's character among many participants, these impressions competed with other factors in their voting decisions rather than determining them automatically. The complexity of voter psychology suggested that dramatic events, while influential, operated within larger frameworks of political identity and policy preference.

Demographic analysis showed that Trump's survival story had particular resonance among older voters, military veterans, and religious conservatives who valued demonstrations of physical courage and interpreted his survival as evidence of divine favor. However, younger voters and college-educated suburbanites, while respecting Trump's response to the assassination attempts, remained more focused on issues like climate change, social policy, and concerns about political rhetoric that the survival narrative couldn't address directly. This demographic variation in response to Trump's martyrdom story created opportunities for both campaigns to target specific voter segments with tailored messages that either emphasized or de-emphasized the assassination attempts' significance.

Polling Predictions

October polling data revealed a presidential race that remained remarkably close despite the dramatic events that had shaped the campaign, with most surveys showing margins within the statistical margin of error that made confident predictions impossible. National polls consistently showed a race separated by fewer than three percentage points, while battleground state polling indicated that the election would likely be determined by turnout differences and late-deciding voters rather than by overwhelming preference for either candidate. The persistence of competitive polling despite

Trump's powerful survival narrative suggested that American voters were capable of weighing multiple factors in their electoral decisions.

Polling analysis also revealed significant challenges in accurately measuring voter sentiment during such an unusual campaign, as traditional survey methods struggled to account for the emotional intensity surrounding Trump's survival story and its impact on voter motivation. Some pollsters reported difficulty in determining whether Trump's martyrdom narrative would primarily affect voter choice or voter turnout, as supporters who were already committed to voting for him became even more enthusiastic while swing voters remained largely unmoved. The uncertainty around turnout models created wide variations in polling predictions that reflected the unprecedented nature of the electoral environment.

The final weeks of polling before Election Day showed a race that defied easy categorization, with Trump's survival narrative providing him with advantages in enthusiasm and fundraising while Harris maintained competitive positions on policy issues and concerns about Trump's fitness for office. State-by-state analysis suggested that the election would likely be determined by turnout differences in a handful of swing states, where Trump's ability to motivate his base through the martyrdom story would compete with Harris's efforts to mobilize voters concerned about reproductive rights, healthcare, and democratic institutions. The polling uncertainty reflected the broader reality that the 2024 election had become unlike any previous contest in American political history.

CHAPTER 16: ELECTION DAY

November 5, 2024, dawned with an electricity in the air that seemed to crackle across the entire American continent. After nearly two years of unprecedented drama—assassination attempts, divine providence narratives, candidate withdrawals, and security threats that had transformed routine campaign events into heavily guarded spectacles—the moment of democratic decision had finally arrived. Polling stations across the nation opened their doors to voters who understood they were participating in what many considered the most consequential election in modern American history, where the choice between Donald Trump and Kamala Harris represented not just different policy preferences but fundamentally different visions of American democracy itself.

The early morning hours brought reports of massive voter turnout that suggested Americans recognized the historic significance of their decision. Lines formed before dawn at polling locations from New Hampshire to Hawaii, as citizens who had witnessed assassination attempts, survival narratives, and religious interpretations of political events came to render their verdict on a campaign unlike any in their lifetimes. The bulletproof glass, the bloodied but defiant photographs, the "Fight! Fight! Fight!" chants, and the martyrdom narratives that had defined Trump's comeback would now be subjected to the ultimate test of democratic legitimacy—the judgment of the American people expressed through their votes.

November 5, 2024

Election Day 2024 began with unprecedented security measures at polling locations across the country, as election officials implemented enhanced protection protocols designed to prevent the kind of political violence that had already twice targeted Trump during the campaign. Federal and local law enforcement agencies coordinated comprehensive security plans that treated voting sites as potential targets for disruption, reflecting how completely the assassination attempts had altered the landscape of American democratic participation. Bulletproof barriers, armed security personnel, and surveillance systems became routine features at polling locations that had historically operated with minimal protection.

The heightened security created an unusual atmosphere at voting sites, where the simple act of casting a ballot felt weighted with historical significance and potential danger. Many voters reported feeling both pride in participating in democracy and concern about their personal safety, reflecting how political violence had infiltrated even the most basic democratic processes. Election workers, who had already faced numerous threats throughout the campaign season, implemented security protocols that balanced accessibility with protection against potential attacks.

Despite security concerns, voter enthusiasm remained extraordinarily high, with early reports suggesting turnout levels that could match or exceed the record participation seen in 2020. Long lines formed at polling locations across swing states, indicating that Americans understood the stakes of their decision and were willing to wait hours to participate in what many viewed as a defining moment for American democracy. The combination of enhanced security and massive turnout created a surreal environment where the most fundamental act of citizenship required extraordinary protective measures.

Early Returns and Predictions

The first exit polls and early returns began painting a picture of an electorate deeply divided not just by partisan preference but by their interpretation of the campaign's extraordinary events. Early data suggested that Trump's survival narrative had indeed mobilized his base in unprecedented numbers, with rural and evangelical voters turning out at rates that exceeded even his successful 2016 campaign. The martyrdom factor appeared to be translating into actual votes, as supporters who viewed Trump's survival as evidence of divine protection demonstrated their faith through electoral participation.

However, Harris's campaign had successfully counter-mobilized different demographic groups, particularly suburban women, young voters, and college-educated Americans who remained concerned about Trump's rhetoric and its impact on democratic institutions. Early returns from urban and suburban areas showed the kind of high Democratic turnout that Harris's team had hoped would offset Trump's advantages in rural regions. The competing mobilization efforts created a complex electoral map where traditional partisan geography was intensified by the emotional dynamics surrounding Trump's assassination survival.

Television networks exercised unusual caution in making early predictions, recognizing that the unprecedented nature of the campaign made traditional electoral models potentially unreliable. The combination of Trump's martyrdom narrative, Harris's historic candidacy, and the security concerns that had dominated the final weeks created analytical challenges that forced media outlets to acknowledge the limitations of their predictive capabilities. Early evening coverage focused more on describing the unique atmosphere surrounding the election rather than confident projections about its outcome.

Swing State Results

The battleground states that had been identified as crucial to the election outcome began reporting results that confirmed pre-election predictions about a closely contested race decided by turnout differences rather than overwhelming preference for either candidate. Pennsylvania, with its nineteen electoral votes and the symbolic significance of being the site of Trump's assassination attempt, became the focal point of national attention as returns showed a competitive race that would likely be determined by Philadelphia suburbs and rural counties where Trump's survival story had particular resonance.

Wisconsin and Michigan, states that had swung from Trump in 2016 to Biden in 2020, showed Trump performing better than in his previous losing effort, suggesting that his martyrdom narrative had indeed helped him recover support among working-class voters who appreciated his willingness to continue campaigning despite mortal danger. The assassination attempt's impact was particularly visible in rural counties where Trump's margins increased significantly compared to 2020, indicating that his survival story had motivated voters who might otherwise have stayed home.

However, Harris demonstrated surprising strength in suburban areas and among college-educated voters who had been repelled by the political violence surrounding Trump's campaign while respecting his personal courage. States like Georgia and Arizona, where demographic changes had been gradually favoring Democrats, showed competitive races that suggested Harris's campaign had successfully navigated the challenge of competing against Trump's powerful survival narrative. The swing state results revealed an electorate capable of weighing multiple factors in their decision-making rather than being determined solely by dramatic campaign events.

The Victory Speech

As election results continued to arrive throughout the evening, it became clear that Donald Trump had achieved what many had considered impossible just months earlier—a return to the presidency after surviving two assassination attempts and overcoming legal challenges that would have ended most political careers. Trump's victory speech, delivered from his campaign headquarters in West Palm Beach, Florida, explicitly connected his electoral triumph to his survival of the July 13th assassination attempt, describing his win as validation of divine providence and American resilience in the face of unprecedented persecution.

"We've achieved the most incredible political thing," Trump declared to a crowd of supporters who had followed his journey from near-death experience to electoral victory. "America has given us an unprecedented and powerful mandate." The speech repeatedly referenced his survival as evidence that God had protected him to complete his mission of restoring American greatness, transforming his assassination experience into proof of his destined leadership. Trump's remarks combined gratitude for his survival with promises of retribution against those who had sought to prevent his return to power through violence and legal persecution.

The victory speech became the culmination of a narrative arc that had begun with gunfire in Butler, Pennsylvania, and ended with electoral triumph in the same state where he had nearly died. Trump's ability to transform victimization into victory, survival into strength, and near-death experience into political resurrection represented one of the most remarkable comebacks in American political history. His speech acknowledged supporters who had stood by him through assassination attempts while warning opponents that their efforts to stop him through violence had only strengthened his resolve and validated his mission to lead America through its challenges.

CHAPTER 17: HOW TRUMP WON

When the final votes were counted on November 5, 2024, Donald Trump had achieved something that seemed nearly impossible just four months earlier when Thomas Matthew Crooks's bullet grazed his ear in Butler, Pennsylvania. Trump's victory was both decisive and comprehensive, encompassing not just the Electoral College triumph that returned him to the White House, but also a popular vote win that had eluded him in both 2016 and 2020. The assassination attempt that could have ended his political career instead became the foundation for one of the most remarkable comebacks in American political history, providing him with a narrative of survival and divine protection that resonated with voters across traditional demographic lines.

The mechanics of Trump's victory revealed how completely the events of July 13th had transformed the electoral landscape, creating new coalitions and motivating previously inactive voters while neutralizing many of the concerns that had limited his appeal in previous campaigns. His survival story had provided him with moral authority that proved difficult for opponents to challenge, while the religious interpretation many voters placed on his narrow escape created emotional connections that transcended typical political loyalties. The result was an electoral triumph that validated not just Trump's political strategy, but the power of authentic human drama to reshape democratic competition in ways that conventional campaigning could never achieve.

Electoral College Breakdown

Trump's path to 312 electoral votes represented a systematic reclamation of states that had abandoned him in 2020, combined with breakthrough victories in traditionally competitive territories where his survival narrative had particular resonance. The former president flipped six crucial states on his way to Electoral College victory: Arizona, Georgia, Michigan, Nevada, Pennsylvania, and Wisconsin. Every other state voted in 2024 as it did in 2020, indicating that Trump's gains were concentrated in the specific battlegrounds where his assassination survival had maximum political impact rather than reflecting a national realignment of partisan preferences.

Pennsylvania's 19 electoral votes carried special symbolic significance, as Trump's victory in the state where he had nearly died provided poetic justice that reinforced the providential narrative central to his campaign. His performance in rural Pennsylvania counties showed dramatic improvement over 2020, suggesting that voters who had witnessed his near-death experience felt personal connections to his survival that translated into electoral support. The state's suburban counties, while still competitive, showed less Democratic intensity than in previous cycles, indicating that Trump's martyrdom story had neutralized some of the opposition that had cost him the state four years earlier.

The southwestern states of Arizona and Nevada demonstrated Trump's ability to expand his coalition beyond the Rust Belt regions where his survival narrative had obvious appeal. His victory in these diverse states suggested that the assassination attempt had created credibility among Hispanic and working-class voters who appreciated displays of physical courage regardless of partisan affiliation. The Electoral College map that emerged from Trump's victory showed a candidate who had successfully leveraged personal trauma into broad-based political appeal that crossed traditional demographic boundaries.

Popular Vote Triumph

Trump's popular vote victory of 77,284,118 votes represented not just a numerical triumph but validation that his survival narrative had indeed connected with the American people in ways that transcended partisan politics. His 49.8 percent vote share, while not quite reaching a majority, represented the highest popular vote total for any Republican candidate in modern history and demonstrated that his assassination survival had expanded his appeal beyond his traditional base. The 3,059,799 more popular votes than he won in 2020 suggested that the martyrdom narrative had motivated new supporters while retaining virtually all of his previous coalition.

The popular vote margin of 1.5 percentage points over Harris, while not overwhelming by historical standards, represented a significant achievement for a candidate who had lost the popular vote in both of his previous campaigns. Trump's ability to finally win more votes than his opponent validated supporter beliefs that he had been denied victory in previous elections through systemic bias rather than genuine unpopularity. The popular vote triumph provided Trump with democratic legitimacy that had been questioned during his first presidency, eliminating arguments about majority rule that had complicated his initial tenure.

Trump's popular vote success was particularly notable given the high turnout environment that typically benefits Democratic candidates, as more than 156 million Americans voted in 2024. His ability to win the most votes despite facing a motivated Democratic opponent suggested that his survival story had fundamentally altered voter perceptions in ways that overcame traditional partisan disadvantages. The popular vote victory became additional evidence for supporters who interpreted Trump's entire political journey as divinely ordained, providing numerical validation for theological interpretations of his assassination survival and electoral triumph.

Demographic Shifts

Trump's 2024 victory revealed significant demographic shifts that reflected the broad appeal of his survival narrative across traditional partisan boundaries, creating a more racially and ethnically diverse coalition than in his previous campaigns. Among Hispanic voters, Trump achieved near parity with Harris (51% Harris, 48% Trump), a dramatic improvement from his 61%-36% loss to Biden in 2020. This shift suggested that Trump's martyrdom story had particular resonance among voters who valued demonstrations of physical courage and personal sacrifice, regardless of their previous partisan loyalties.

Trump's support among Black voters increased from 8% in 2020 to 15% in 2024, representing his best performance with African American voters in any of his three presidential campaigns. While still a minority of Black support, this improvement indicated that Trump's survival narrative had created credibility among voters who might disagree with his policies but could respect his willingness to continue campaigning despite mortal danger. The demographic shift was most pronounced among Black men, suggesting that displays of physical courage resonated particularly strongly with male voters across racial lines.

The Trump coalition also showed continued strength among white working-class voters while making inroads with suburban women who had previously opposed him but were moved by his response to the assassination attempts. Trump won voters living in rural areas by 40 points (69%-29%), higher than his margins in 2020 or 2016, indicating that his survival story had intensified existing loyalties while attracting new supporters. These demographic shifts revealed an electorate capable of weighing character demonstrations alongside policy preferences, with Trump's assassination survival providing evidence of personal qualities that transcended typical political considerations.

The Coalition That Delivered

The coalition that delivered Trump's victory combined his traditional base of rural, white, and evangelical voters with significant new support from demographics that had previously been skeptical of his candidacy but were moved by his survival narrative and response to assassination attempts. Religious voters formed the core of Trump's expanded coalition, with nearly two-thirds of voters who attend religious services monthly or more (64%) voting for Trump. The assassination attempt had provided theological validation for evangelical supporters while attracting religious voters from other traditions who interpreted his survival as evidence of divine favor.

Trump's campaign thesis of "max out the men and hold the women" proved successful as he significantly improved his performance among male voters across racial and ethnic lines while limiting his losses among women through the credibility generated by his survival story. Working-class men, military veterans, and voters in rural communities responded particularly strongly to Trump's demonstration of physical courage under fire, viewing his continued campaigning as evidence of the kind of leadership America needed during dangerous times. These voters formed the enthusiastic core of rally attendance that created the visual spectacle of Trump's survival narrative.

The coalition also included significant numbers of voters who had not participated in previous elections but were motivated by Trump's martyrdom story to engage in democratic participation for the first time. Focus groups revealed that many Trump voters described their support as responding to his personal sacrifice rather than policy agreement, suggesting that authentic human drama had created political loyalties that transcended traditional partisan calculations. This expanded coalition of survival narrative supporters, combined with Trump's traditional base, created the mathematical foundation for his Electoral College and popular vote victories.

CHAPTER 18: THE ASSASSINATION ATTEMPT FACTOR

The question that would define post-election analysis for decades to come was deceptively simple: How much did the assassination attempts actually contribute to Donald Trump's victory? While Trump's survival narrative had dominated campaign coverage and created powerful emotional connections with supporters, separating its electoral impact from other factors—economic concerns, partisan polarization, candidate quality, and traditional voting patterns— proved extraordinarily complex. The assassination attempt had occurred during a period when Trump was already gaining ground against Biden, making it difficult to isolate the survival story's specific contribution to his ultimate triumph over Kamala Harris.

Yet comprehensive polling data, voter interviews, and demographic analysis revealed that the events of July 13th had indeed played a crucial role in reshaping the electoral landscape, though not always in ways that conventional political wisdom might have predicted. The assassination attempt's impact operated through multiple channels—direct sympathy for Trump's survival, religious interpretations of divine intervention, admiration for his courage under fire, and increased motivation among supporters who viewed his continued campaigning as heroic sacrifice. Understanding the assassination attempt factor required examining not just immediate polling changes, but the deeper psychological and spiritual connections that transformed routine political support into something approaching religious devotion among significant segments of the American electorate.

Polling Data Analysis

Comprehensive analysis of polling trends throughout the 2024 campaign revealed that Trump's assassination survival had indeed provided measurable electoral benefits, though the impact was more complex and sustained than the typical convention bounces or temporary sympathy effects that characterize most campaign events. Most people (58%) believed the attempted assassination would increase Trump's odds of winning, with Republicans (75%) more likely than Independents (52%) and Democrats (47%) to predict electoral benefits. This widespread expectation of political advantage suggested that voters recognized the assassination attempt as a potentially decisive campaign moment.

However, immediate polling after the Butler shooting showed surprisingly modest short-term gains, with Trump and Biden remaining locked in statistical ties despite the dramatic nature of the survival story. The Reuters/Ipsos polling fielded after the assassination attempt showed Trump with only a slight lead among registered voters (43% to Biden's 41%), falling within the poll's margin of error. This limited immediate bounce reflected the highly polarized nature of the electorate, where even extraordinary events like assassination attempts struggled to move voters across partisan lines in significant numbers.

The more significant polling impact became visible over time, as Trump's survival narrative was reinforced through convention appearances, campaign messaging, and sustained media coverage that kept the assassination attempt in voters' minds throughout the campaign. Tracking polls showed gradual but consistent improvement in Trump's favorability ratings and voter enthusiasm measures, suggesting that the martyrdom story created cumulative effects that traditional polling snapshots might miss. The polling data indicated that the assassination attempt's primary benefit was motivating Trump's existing supporters rather than converting opponents, creating turnout advantages that proved decisive in closely contested swing states.

Voter Interviews and Motivation

In-depth interviews with Trump voters conducted after the election revealed that the assassination attempt had functioned as a powerful motivational factor that transformed routine political support into passionate advocacy for many supporters. Focus groups consistently showed that voters who had planned to support Trump regardless of the assassination attempt became significantly more enthusiastic about their choice after witnessing his survival and defiant response. Many described feeling personally connected to Trump's suffering in ways that transcended typical candidate-voter relationships, viewing his continued campaigning as evidence of selfless dedication to their cause.

Perhaps more significantly, voter interviews identified substantial numbers of Americans who had been politically inactive or undecided before the assassination attempt but were motivated to vote for Trump specifically because of his survival story. These "assassination converts" described being moved by Trump's courage under fire and his immediate return to campaigning despite obvious personal danger. Their testimonials revealed that authentic demonstrations of character could indeed influence electoral behavior in ways that policy positions or campaign messaging could not achieve, providing validation for Trump's instinctive decision to emphasize strength rather than victimization.

The interviews also revealed important demographic variations in how voters interpreted and responded to Trump's survival story, with military veterans, rural Americans, and religious conservatives showing particularly strong emotional connections to his martyrdom narrative. These groups consistently described the assassination attempt as validating their existing beliefs about Trump's exceptional leadership qualities while providing additional motivation for electoral participation. The depth of emotional response among these core constituencies helped explain Trump's ability to generate record-breaking rally attendance and fundraising levels throughout the remainder of the campaign.

The Sympathy Vote Reality

Analysis of voting patterns and electoral behavior revealed that traditional concepts of "sympathy votes" inadequately captured the complex ways that Trump's assassination survival influenced electoral decision-making. Rather than generating temporary pity that might fade over time, the assassination attempt created lasting admiration for Trump's response to crisis that enhanced his credibility on leadership qualities that many voters considered essential for presidential effectiveness. Polls showed that 47% of voters believed Trump's response to the shooting demonstrated presidential temperament, suggesting that the assassination attempt had provided evidence of character rather than merely generating sympathy.

The sympathy vote concept also failed to account for the religious and spiritual interpretations that many voters placed on Trump's survival, which created theological rather than emotional motivations for electoral support. Survey data revealed that 66% of registered Republicans believed Trump was "favored by divine

113

providence or God's will," indicating that many supporters viewed their votes as acts of faith rather than expressions of sympathy. This religious dimension transformed electoral participation into spiritual obligation for significant segments of Trump's coalition, creating motivation that extended far beyond temporary emotional responses.

International comparisons of political violence and electoral outcomes suggested that Trump's ability to convert assassination survival into lasting political advantage was historically unusual, as most politicians who survive attacks experience only brief polling improvements that dissipate as normal political competition resumes. Trump's sustained benefits from the assassination attempt reflected both his unique ability to craft compelling narratives from personal trauma and the particular resonance his survival story found within American political culture. The sympathy vote reality proved to be less about pity and more about respect, less about temporary emotion and more about permanent credibility that enhanced Trump's political brand in fundamental ways.

Divine Intervention Beliefs

The religious interpretation of Trump's assassination survival emerged as one of the most significant factors in understanding the electoral impact of July 13th, as millions of Americans viewed his narrow escape as evidence of supernatural protection that validated his political mission. Polling data consistently showed that approximately one-third of Americans agreed that Trump had been "favored by divine providence or God's will," with much higher percentages among evangelical Christians and regular churchgoers who formed crucial elements of his electoral coalition. These divine intervention beliefs created political loyalties that transcended typical partisan calculations, transforming electoral support into religious devotion.

The theological framework surrounding Trump's survival provided his campaign with messaging opportunities that connected with voters' deepest spiritual convictions while offering explanations for his political resurrection that secular analyses could not provide. Campaign events increasingly resembled religious revivals, with prayer, Christian music, and explicitly providential language about America's spiritual destiny becoming standard features of Trump rallies. This fusion of politics and theology created unprecedented enthusiasm among religious voters who understood their electoral participation as obedience to divine command rather than mere civic engagement.

The divine intervention narrative also provided Trump supporters with theological justification for political actions and rhetoric that might otherwise seem extreme or un-Christian, as opposition to someone protected by God could be framed as opposition to divine will itself. This religious interpretation of partisan politics elevated normal democratic competition to the level of spiritual warfare, making compromise or peaceful coexistence with political opponents increasingly difficult to justify on theological grounds. The widespread belief in divine intervention surrounding Trump's survival demonstrated both the power of religious conviction in American politics and the potential dangers of sanctifying partisan political positions with claims of supernatural authority.

CHAPTER 19: THE NEW TRUMP PRESIDENCY

On January 20, 2025, Donald Trump raised his right hand to take the presidential oath of office, the same hand he had raised in defiant victory on July 13, 2024, moments after surviving an assassin's bullet. The inauguration ceremony itself bore the unmistakable marks of a presidency born from political violence and divine intervention narratives, with security measures that resembled a military operation more than a traditional democratic celebration. Bulletproof glass surrounded the inaugural platform, Secret Service snipers occupied every nearby rooftop, and the National Mall was divided into secure zones that reflected the ongoing threats facing a president who had survived two assassination attempts during his campaign.

Trump's inaugural address explicitly connected his survival to his return to power, describing his presidency as a divinely ordained mission to restore America after surviving persecution that would have destroyed lesser leaders. The speech marked not just the beginning of his second term, but the culmination of a political resurrection that had transformed near-death experience into ultimate victory. The president who took the oath that January morning was fundamentally different from the man who had first assumed office in 2017—shaped by assassination attempts, strengthened by survival, and convinced that Providence had preserved him for this historic moment of American renewal.

Inauguration Day

The 2025 presidential inauguration represented the most heavily secured ceremony in American history, with security arrangements that reflected both the ongoing threats against Trump's life and the symbolic importance of peacefully transferring power to a leader who had survived multiple assassination attempts. The Capitol building was surrounded by bulletproof barriers, while military personnel and law enforcement agencies implemented protection protocols that treated the event as both celebration and potential target. The visible security apparatus served as reminder that American democracy was operating under unprecedented threat conditions.

Trump's inaugural address lasted 47 minutes and repeatedly referenced his assassination survival as evidence that God had protected him to complete his mission of American restoration. "We have been tested by fire and emerged stronger," Trump declared, explicitly connecting his personal survival to national resilience. The speech combined traditional inaugural themes of unity and renewal with more confrontational language about defeating enemies who had sought to prevent his return through violence and persecution.

The ceremony attracted crowds that campaign officials claimed exceeded attendance at Trump's first inauguration, though independent verification proved difficult due to security restrictions that limited public access to traditional viewing areas. International dignitaries attended in unprecedented numbers, with many world leaders expressing fascination with Trump's political resurrection and desire to understand how assassination survival had translated into electoral victory. The inauguration became global spectacle that

117

demonstrated both American democratic resilience and the extraordinary circumstances surrounding Trump's return to power.

Security Transformed

Trump's presidency began with security arrangements that fundamentally altered how American presidents would be protected, as the Secret Service implemented comprehensive reforms designed to prevent the kind of assassination attempts that had twice nearly succeeded during the campaign. The White House grounds were enhanced with advanced surveillance technology, while Trump's travel required security measures that exceeded even wartime presidential protection. Every public appearance involved bulletproof barriers, extensive advance work, and counter-surveillance operations that treated routine presidential activities as potential assassination opportunities.

The transformation extended beyond physical security to include cybersecurity enhancements, communication protocol changes, and threat assessment procedures that reflected lessons learned from the Butler and Florida incidents. Secret Service personnel levels were increased dramatically, while coordination with local law enforcement agencies was systematized to prevent the communication failures that had contributed to July 13th's near-catastrophe. These changes represented the most significant evolution in presidential protection since the Secret Service assumed responsibility for presidential security in 1901.

International security cooperation also expanded as foreign intelligence services shared information about potential threats against Trump, recognizing that his survival had global implications for democratic stability and international relations. The enhanced security created unprecedented constraints on presidential accessibility while ensuring that Trump could continue performing his duties without the constant fear of assassination that had characterized his campaign period. The security transformation became permanent feature of American presidency, establishing protocols that would protect future presidents regardless of their individual threat profiles.

Policy Implications

Trump's survival narrative profoundly influenced his presidential agenda, as policies were consistently framed through the lens of a leader who had literally sacrificed for American values and deserved public support for his continued service despite ongoing danger. His legislative priorities emphasized themes of strength, security, and national resilience that connected directly to his assassination survival story, while opponents found it politically difficult to challenge initiatives proposed by someone who had been targeted for political murder. The martyrdom narrative provided Trump with political capital that translated into congressional support and public approval for controversial policies.

Immigration enforcement, border security, and national defense spending received enhanced priority as Trump argued that his survival demonstrated America's need for leaders willing to face personal danger to protect national interests. His policy proposals consistently emphasized confronting enemies both foreign and domestic who had proven their willingness to resort to violence against American democratic institutions. The assassination attempts became justification for expanded executive powers and

119

enhanced security measures that previous presidents might have found politically impossible to implement.

Trump's economic agenda also reflected his survival narrative, with policies designed to reward the working-class Americans who had supported him through assassination attempts and electoral victory. Tax cuts, regulatory reform, and trade policies were presented as fulfilling promises made to supporters who had demonstrated extraordinary loyalty during his time of greatest danger. The policy implications of Trump's survival extended beyond specific legislative items to encompass a governing philosophy that viewed presidential authority as validated by personal sacrifice and democratic mandate earned through survived persecution.

A Changed Man?

Those closest to President Trump reported that his assassination survival had indeed fundamentally altered his personality and approach to presidential leadership, though whether these changes represented genuine transformation or strategic adaptation remained subject to debate among observers and critics. Trump's public statements displayed greater emphasis on themes of gratitude, divine purpose, and national unity, suggesting that his near-death experience had provided perspective on mortality and legacy that influenced his presidential priorities. His rhetoric, while still combative toward opponents, incorporated more explicit religious language and references to providential protection.

However, Trump's governing style retained many characteristics that had defined his first presidency, including impulsive decision-making, conflict with media outlets, and confrontational approaches to political opposition. Critics argued that his survival narrative had actually intensified his combative instincts by providing moral justification for aggressive tactics against enemies who had literally tried to kill him. The assassination attempts seemed to have reinforced Trump's existing worldview about persecution and victimization rather than moderating his political approach.

The question of whether Trump had been fundamentally changed by his survival remained unanswered during his presidency's early months, as observers struggled to separate authentic personal transformation from strategic political positioning. What seemed certain was that the assassination attempts had provided Trump with unshakeable confidence in his political destiny and divine protection that influenced every aspect of his presidential performance. Whether this confidence would lead to more effective leadership or dangerous overreach would become one of the defining questions of his second term.

CHAPTER 20: SECRET SERVICE REFORMS

The assassination attempt at Butler, Pennsylvania, had exposed systemic failures in presidential protection that demanded immediate and comprehensive reform of the Secret Service's operational procedures, resource allocation, and institutional culture. The agency that had been created to prevent exactly the kind of attack that Thomas Matthew Crooks nearly carried out found itself facing the most serious crisis of confidence in its modern history, with bipartisan congressional pressure demanding accountability and fundamental changes to ensure such failures could never happen again. The reforms that emerged from the Butler incident would represent the most significant transformation of presidential protection since the agency's creation, touching everything from communication protocols to threat assessment procedures.

The process of reform was complicated by the need to balance enhanced security with democratic accessibility, as the assassination attempt had demonstrated that traditional approaches to candidate protection were inadequate for the modern threat environment while also revealing the political and practical costs of turning every campaign event into a military-style operation. The Secret Service faced the challenge of learning from its failures without overcorrecting in ways that would fundamentally alter the character of American democratic participation, requiring surgical precision in implementing changes that would enhance protection without destroying the openness that defines American political culture.

What Went Wrong

The comprehensive investigations into the Butler assassination attempt revealed a cascade of institutional failures that went far beyond individual mistakes to encompass systemic problems with communication, coordination, resource allocation, and threat assessment that had been building within the Secret Service for years. The most fundamental failure involved the fragmented command structure that prevented local law enforcement's observations about Thomas Matthew Crooks's suspicious behavior from reaching the federal agents directly responsible for Trump's protection, creating information silos at the precise moment when rapid coordination could have saved lives.

Resource denials represented another critical failure, as the Secret Service headquarters had systematically rejected requests from Trump's protective detail for enhanced security measures despite mounting intelligence about Iranian assassination plots and increased domestic threats. The agency's "history of denials" for additional security assets during Trump's campaign reflected budgetary priorities and bureaucratic resistance that prioritized cost-cutting over comprehensive protection, leaving agents in the field without the tools they needed to address evolving threat environments.

Personnel and planning failures compounded these systemic problems, with critical coordination responsibilities assigned to agents unfamiliar with local arrangements just days before the rally. The security room agent responsible for communication between agencies was assigned to Butler only two days before the event and discovered the existence of separate command posts only through overheard conversations. These last-minute assignments violated basic security principles while ensuring that critical functions would be performed by personnel without adequate preparation or local knowledge.

Systemic Changes Implemented

The Secret Service implemented comprehensive reforms designed to address every identified failure from the Butler incident, beginning with complete restructuring of communication protocols to ensure seamless information sharing between federal and local law enforcement agencies. New standardized communication systems eliminated the separate command posts that had created dangerous information gaps, while real-time intelligence sharing platforms ensured that threat information would reach protective agents immediately regardless of its original source.

Resource allocation procedures were fundamentally reformed to prioritize threat-based security decisions over budgetary considerations, with enhanced funding for counter-sniper teams, counter-assault units, and advanced surveillance technology that would be deployed based on intelligence assessments rather than cost constraints. The agency established new protocols requiring that all outdoor events for protected individuals receive comprehensive perimeter security, while counter-drone systems and enhanced crowd screening became standard rather than optional protective measures.

Personnel management reforms eliminated last-minute assignments of critical security roles while establishing minimum experience and training requirements for agents assigned to coordinate multi-agency operations. New advance planning procedures required security assessments to be completed weeks rather than days before protected events, while mandatory briefings ensured that all personnel understood their roles within the broader security apparatus. These changes represented the most significant operational reforms in Secret Service history, fundamentally altering how the agency approached its protective mission.

Congressional Oversight

The Task Force on the Attempted Assassination of Donald J. Trump's comprehensive investigation established new frameworks for congressional oversight of Secret Service operations that would prevent future institutional complacency while ensuring ongoing accountability for protective failures. The task force's final report, released on December 10, 2024, provided 46 transcripts from interviews with local, state, and federal officials while offering detailed recommendations for preventing similar security breakdowns in future protective operations.

Congressional oversight reforms included mandatory reporting requirements that would inform relevant committees about threat assessments, resource requests, and security protocols for all major protective operations. The Secret Service would be required to justify resource allocation decisions and explain how threat intelligence influenced security planning, creating transparency that had been absent during the Butler preparations. Regular congressional briefings on evolving threat environments would ensure that lawmakers understood the challenges facing protective agencies while providing oversight of reform implementation.

The legislation emerging from the congressional investigation also established independent review mechanisms for evaluating Secret Service performance during significant protective events, ensuring that future failures would be identified and addressed before they could contribute to successful attacks. Congressional funding for Secret Service operations was restructured to prioritize threat-based resource allocation while providing the agency with flexibility to respond to evolving security challenges without bureaucratic delays that had contributed to the Butler failures.

Future Protection Protocols

The new protection protocols established in response to the Butler assassination attempt created comprehensive security frameworks that would govern presidential and candidate protection for decades to come, fundamentally altering how American political leaders would interact with the public while maintaining democratic accessibility. Bulletproof barriers became mandatory for all outdoor events involving current or former presidents, while enhanced counter-sniper capabilities and advanced surveillance technology were deployed at every significant political gathering.

Threat assessment procedures were completely overhauled to incorporate real-time intelligence analysis, social media monitoring, and behavioral assessment capabilities that would identify potential attackers before they could position themselves for attacks. The new protocols required comprehensive background investigations of all individuals with access to protected venues, while advanced screening technology and expanded security perimeters pushed potential threats much further from protected persons.

International coordination became standard practice as the Secret Service established formal intelligence-sharing relationships with allied security services, recognizing that threats against American political leaders increasingly originated from foreign sources requiring global surveillance and prevention efforts. These future protection protocols represented permanent changes to American political culture, ensuring that the kind of security failures that enabled the Butler assassination attempt could never be repeated while acknowledging that democratic participation would occur within new frameworks designed to prevent political violence from succeeding.

CHAPTER 21: POLITICAL VIOLENCE IN AMERICA

The assassination attempts against Donald Trump in 2024 forced Americans to confront an uncomfortable truth about their democracy: political violence, once considered an aberration from a distant and less civilized past, had become a persistent feature of contemporary American political life. The bullets fired at Trump in Butler, Pennsylvania, and the rifle aimed at him in Florida were not isolated incidents but rather the most dramatic manifestations of a broader pattern of political violence that had been escalating for years. From the January 6th Capitol attack to threats against election workers, from the assault on Nancy Pelosi's husband to plots against governors and judges, American politics had entered an era where violence and the threat of violence shaped democratic participation in unprecedented ways.

Understanding Trump's assassination attempts required placing them within this larger context of American political violence, recognizing that while the specific targeting of a former president represented an escalation, the underlying conditions that made such attacks possible had been developing for decades. The normalization of violent rhetoric, the proliferation of military-grade weapons, the erosion of shared democratic norms, and the tribal polarization that characterized modern American politics had created an environment where assassination attempts were not shocking anomalies but predictable outcomes of systemic dysfunction. The question facing American democracy was whether Trump's survival would serve as a wake-up call leading to meaningful reforms, or whether political violence would continue escalating until it fundamentally altered the character of democratic governance in the United States.

Historical Context

Political violence has been a recurring feature of American history since the nation's founding, with four presidential assassinations and numerous additional attempts demonstrating that democratic institutions have never been completely immune to violent disruption. The assassinations of Abraham Lincoln in 1865, James Garfield in 1881, William McKinley in 1901, and John F. Kennedy in 1963 each occurred during periods of intense political polarization and social upheaval, suggesting that political violence often emerges from deeper societal tensions rather than individual pathology alone.

The modern era of political violence began with the turbulent 1960s, when assassinations claimed not only President Kennedy but also civil rights leader Martin Luther King Jr. and presidential candidate Robert F. Kennedy in 1968. The decade also witnessed the attempted assassination of Alabama Governor George Wallace in 1972, creating a pattern of political violence that seemed to target leaders across the political spectrum. These attacks prompted significant improvements in protective services and security protocols that successfully prevented political assassinations for over four decades.

However, the assassination attempt on President Ronald Reagan in 1981 demonstrated that even enhanced security measures could not completely eliminate the threat of political violence, while the September 11, 2001 terrorist attacks revealed new forms of political violence that traditional protective measures were not designed to address. The historical context of American political violence suggested that Trump's assassination attempts were part of a recurring pattern rather than unprecedented events, though the

129

specific circumstances of modern threats reflected contemporary challenges that previous generations had not faced.

The New Normal?

The frequency and intensity of political threats in the 2020s suggested that American democracy might be entering a new phase where political violence becomes routine rather than exceptional, fundamentally altering how democratic participation occurs and how political leaders interact with the public. Since the 2020 election, thousands of death threats had been directed at election workers, officials, and their families, while multiple plots against governors, judges, and members of Congress demonstrated that political violence was no longer limited to attempts against presidents or presidential candidates.

The normalization of violent rhetoric in political discourse had created permission structures that made actual violence seem like logical extensions of political competition rather than violations of democratic norms. Social media platforms amplified the most extreme voices while creating echo chambers that reinforced beliefs about the existential nature of political differences, making compromise appear treasonous and violence seem patriotic. This rhetorical environment had contributed to multiple incidents of political violence, from the 2017 shooting of Republican members of Congress to the 2022 attack on Nancy Pelosi's husband.

The question of whether political violence had become America's "new normal" reflected deeper concerns about democratic resilience and institutional capacity to contain extremist threats. Polling data consistently showed that significant minorities of Americans across the political spectrum believed political violence could be justified under certain circumstances, while majorities expressed concern that democracy itself was under threat. The widespread acceptance of political violence as potentially legitimate represented a fundamental shift in American political culture that posed existential challenges to democratic governance.

Preventing Future Attacks

Preventing future political assassinations and attacks required comprehensive approaches that addressed both immediate security vulnerabilities and the underlying social conditions that produced political violence, recognizing that protective measures alone could not solve systemic problems that encouraged violent solutions to political disagreements. Enhanced security protocols implemented after Trump's assassination attempts represented necessary but insufficient responses to threats that emerged from broader patterns of political polarization and extremist radicalization.

Law enforcement agencies expanded their focus on domestic terrorism and political violence, developing new capabilities for monitoring online extremist communities and identifying individuals who might transition from violent rhetoric to actual attacks. These efforts included improved coordination between federal and local agencies, enhanced information sharing about potential threats, and specialized training for recognizing the warning signs that preceded political violence. However, these security measures operated within constitutional constraints that limited surveillance capabilities while protecting civil liberties.

More fundamental prevention efforts required addressing the root causes of political violence through education, media literacy, and political reforms designed to reduce the polarization and zero-sum thinking that contributed to extremist radicalization. Some experts advocated for social media regulation, campaign finance reform, and electoral changes that might reduce the incentives for extreme rhetoric and behavior. Others emphasized the importance of political leadership that consistently condemned violence while modeling democratic norms and respectful disagreement, recognizing that prevention ultimately depended on cultural changes that valued democratic participation over tribal warfare.

Democracy Under Threat

The assassination attempts against Trump crystallized broader concerns about American democracy's vulnerability to violent disruption, as political scientists and international observers noted troubling parallels between contemporary American political violence and patterns that had undermined democratic institutions in other nations. The willingness of significant portions of the population to accept or encourage political violence represented a fundamental challenge to democratic legitimacy that went beyond specific security threats to encompass questions about whether American democratic culture remained viable.

International democracy indices had already downgraded American democratic rankings due to concerns about electoral integrity, political polarization, and institutional erosion that preceded Trump's assassination attempts but were reinforced by the violence surrounding his campaigns. The fact that two separate individuals had attempted to assassinate a former president within months of each other suggested systematic problems with American political culture that technical security solutions could not address, requiring fundamental reforms to restore democratic norms and peaceful competition.

The threat to democracy extended beyond immediate concerns about political violence to encompass the broader implications of operating democratic institutions under siege conditions, where bulletproof barriers, military-style security, and constant threat assessments became routine features of political participation. This militarization of democratic life risked fundamentally altering the character of American political culture while potentially discouraging civic engagement among citizens who viewed political participation as dangerous. The ultimate test of American democracy would be whether it could address the conditions that produced political violence while maintaining the openness and accessibility that defined democratic governance.

CHAPTER 22: THE MAKING OF A POLITICAL LEGEND

The transformation of Donald Trump from controversial political figure to legendary survivor represents one of the most remarkable character arcs in American political history, rivaling the mythic narratives that have surrounded figures like Abraham Lincoln, Franklin Roosevelt, and Ronald Reagan. The bullet that grazed Trump's ear on July 13, 2024, did more than create a physical wound—it created a legend that would be studied, debated, and remembered long after the specific policy details of his presidency had faded from public memory. The image of Trump rising from behind the podium, blood streaming down his face, fist raised in defiance against the backdrop of the American flag, achieved instant iconic status that transcended partisan politics to become part of the broader American story.

The making of this political legend involved the convergence of authentic human drama, masterful narrative construction, and deep cultural currents in American society that valued displays of physical courage and divine protection. Trump's instinctive response to mortal danger—his refusal to be evacuated immediately, his insistence on facing the crowd, his defiant "Fight! Fight! Fight!" cry—provided the raw material for a survival story that resonated with fundamental American values about resilience, determination, and strength in the face of adversity. The legend that emerged from Butler, Pennsylvania, would influence American political culture for generations, establishing new templates for how leaders respond to crisis while creating lasting changes in how Americans understand the relationship between personal character and political authority.

Trump's Place in History

Donald Trump's survival of assassination attempts secured his place in American history as a figure who transcended ordinary political categories to become something approaching a folk hero, joining the ranks of leaders who had faced mortal peril in service of their political convictions. His unique position as the only former president to survive multiple assassination attempts during a campaign for re-election created historical precedents that scholars would study for decades, while his successful conversion of near-death experiences into electoral victory established new paradigms for political resilience and narrative construction.

Trump's historical significance extended beyond his policy achievements or political controversies to encompass his role in demonstrating how authentic human drama could reshape democratic competition in the modern media age. His assassination survival provided evidence that voters remained capable of responding to displays of genuine character under pressure, suggesting that democratic politics had not become completely artificial or manufactured despite the dominance of professional campaign management and digital manipulation.

The historical assessment of Trump's presidency would inevitably be influenced by the extraordinary circumstances of his return to power, as his survival narrative provided context for understanding his subsequent policy decisions and political behavior. Historians would debate whether his assassination attempts represented random acts of violence or systematic attempts to undermine democratic processes, while his response to those attacks would be analyzed as either authentic leadership or calculated political theater. Regardless of these interpretations, Trump's place in history

135

as a survivor who transformed victimization into victory was permanently established by the events of July 13, 2024.

The Survival Narrative

The survival narrative that emerged from Trump's assassination attempts became a powerful cultural touchstone that influenced how Americans understood leadership, resilience, and the relationship between personal character and political authority. The story's essential elements—the near-miss that measured survival in millimeters, the immediate defiant response that prioritized strength over safety, the visible evidence of bloodshed in service of political conviction—created a compelling tale that satisfied deep human needs for heroic narratives in political life.

The narrative's power derived partly from its authenticity, as Trump's response to genuine mortal danger provided evidence of character that no amount of campaign staging could manufacture. The blood on his face, the fist raised toward the crowd, the immediate return to campaigning despite obvious personal risk—these elements created credibility that transcended typical political messaging while providing supporters with tangible proof of their leader's exceptional qualities. The survival story became central to Trump's political identity in ways that policy positions or electoral victories could not achieve.

The cultural resonance of Trump's survival narrative reflected broader American fascination with stories of triumph over adversity, individual resilience in the face of overwhelming odds, and the idea that exceptional leaders emerge from exceptional circumstances.

The narrative tapped into religious themes about divine protection and secular themes about physical courage, creating cross-cutting appeal that reached different segments of the population for different reasons. This multi-layered narrative structure ensured that Trump's survival story would remain compelling to diverse audiences long after the immediate political circumstances that created it had passed.

Cultural Impact

Trump's assassination survival created lasting changes in American political culture that extended far beyond electoral politics to influence how Americans understood the relationship between violence, leadership, and democratic participation. The normalization of bulletproof barriers at political events, the acceptance of military-style security for candidates, and the integration of survival narratives into campaign messaging represented permanent shifts in how democratic politics would be conducted in the United States.

The cultural impact also included the elevation of physical courage as a criterion for political leadership, as Trump's willingness to continue campaigning despite obvious personal danger created new expectations for how politicians should respond to threats. Future candidates would be measured against Trump's standard of continuing to engage with voters despite security risks, while displays of caution or concern for personal safety might be interpreted as weakness or lack of commitment to public service.

Perhaps most significantly, Trump's survival narrative contributed to the ongoing militarization of American political rhetoric, where political competition was increasingly framed in terms of warfare, survival, and existential struggle rather than policy disagreement or democratic competition. The cultural fascination with Trump's near-death experience reinforced tendencies to view politics through dramatic rather than deliberative frameworks, potentially making future political violence more likely by celebrating the heroic narratives that could emerge from such attacks.

Long-term Political Consequences

The long-term political consequences of Trump's assassination survival extended beyond his personal electoral success to encompass fundamental changes in how American democracy would function, as the integration of violence and survival narratives into mainstream political competition created new dynamics that would influence political behavior for decades. The demonstration that assassination attempts could provide political advantages rather than ending careers created perverse incentives that might encourage future political violence while changing how politicians calculated risks and benefits of public engagement.

Trump's successful conversion of victimization into electoral victory established new templates for political resilience that future leaders would attempt to emulate, though without the authentic drama that made Trump's survival narrative compelling. The expectation that political leaders should demonstrate exceptional courage under fire while maintaining accessibility to voters created tensions that would complicate security planning and democratic participation for generations.

The religious interpretation that many Americans placed on Trump's survival also created lasting changes in how faith and politics intersected, as the providential narrative surrounding his assassination attempts reinforced beliefs about divine intervention in American political life. This theological framework for understanding electoral outcomes would influence how religious voters approached future elections while potentially making political opposition seem like opposition to divine will, creating dangerous precedents for mixing religious authority with partisan political positions.

CONCLUSION

On the evening of July 13, 2024, as the sun set over the Butler Farm Show Grounds in Pennsylvania, Donald Trump was eight minutes into what seemed like another routine campaign rally. By 6:11 PM, when Thomas Matthew Crooks's rifle fire shattered the summer air, the trajectory of American political history had been forever altered. The eight seconds of chaos that followed—from the first gunshot to Trump's defiant "Fight! Fight! Fight!" cry—contained more political consequence than most presidential terms achieve in four years. A bullet that missed its target by approximately two inches became the catalyst for one of the most remarkable political comebacks in democratic history.

This book has traced the extraordinary journey from assassination attempt to electoral triumph, revealing how authentic human drama under the most extreme circumstances could reshape political competition in ways that conventional campaigning never could. Trump's survival of not one but two assassination attempts, combined with his instinctive response to mortal danger, created a narrative of resilience and divine protection that resonated with voters across traditional partisan boundaries. The blood streaming down his face, the fist raised in defiance, the immediate return to campaigning despite obvious personal risk—these authentic displays of courage under fire provided credibility that no amount of advertising dollars could purchase.

The Transformation of American Politics

The 2024 election will be remembered as the moment when American politics fully embraced the reality that violence and the threat of violence had become permanent features of democratic competition. The bulletproof glass barriers that became standard at Trump rallies, the military-style security that surrounded every campaign event, and the constant presence of counter-sniper teams represented more than temporary precautions—they marked the militarization of American democratic participation in ways that will shape political culture for generations.

Yet paradoxically, these enhanced security measures coincided with some of the largest and most enthusiastic political crowds in American history, as Trump's survival narrative drew supporters who wanted to witness firsthand a leader who had literally shed blood for his cause. The assassination attempt had transformed routine campaign events into historical moments that Americans felt compelled to experience personally, creating a level of political engagement that transcended typical electoral enthusiasm to approach something resembling religious devotion.

The transformation extended beyond campaign dynamics to encompass fundamental changes in how Americans understood the relationship between personal character and political authority. Trump's willingness to continue campaigning despite obvious personal danger created new standards for political courage while demonstrating that voters remained capable of responding to authentic displays of leadership under pressure. The survival story provided evidence that democratic politics had not become completely artificial or manufactured, offering hope that genuine human qualities could still triumph over professional campaign management and digital manipulation.

The Divine Providence Factor

Perhaps no aspect of Trump's victory was more significant—or more troubling—than the widespread belief among his supporters that divine intervention had preserved his life for the specific purpose of restoring American greatness. The providential interpretation of his assassination survival created political loyalties that transcended typical partisan calculations, transforming electoral support into religious devotion among significant segments of the American electorate. Campaign rallies increasingly resembled religious revivals, while opposition to Trump could be framed as opposition to God's will itself.

This fusion of faith and politics created unprecedented enthusiasm among religious voters while establishing dangerous precedents for mixing divine authority with partisan political positions. The theological framework surrounding Trump's survival reinforced beliefs about supernatural intervention in American political life, creating expectations that future elections would similarly reflect divine will rather than democratic choice. The long-term implications of sanctifying partisan political positions with claims of supernatural protection remain one of the most concerning legacies of the 2024 election.

The divine providence narrative also revealed the continuing power of religious conviction in American political culture, demonstrating that spiritual interpretations of political events could motivate voter behavior in ways that secular analyses often underestimated. Trump's ability to integrate his survival story into broader themes of American exceptionalism and religious destiny showed how traditional religious values could be mobilized for contemporary

142

political purposes, creating coalitions that combined theological conviction with partisan loyalty.

The Price of Political Legend

Trump's transformation from assassination target to political legend came at significant costs that extended far beyond his personal experience to encompass the broader health of American democratic institutions. The normalization of political violence as a routine feature of electoral competition created permission structures that made future attacks more likely while establishing heroic narratives that could emerge from such violence. The demonstration that assassination attempts could provide political advantages rather than ending careers created perverse incentives that threatened to encourage rather than deter political violence.

The cultural celebration of Trump's survival, while understandable given the extraordinary circumstances, contributed to the ongoing militarization of American political rhetoric where competition was increasingly framed in terms of warfare, survival, and existential struggle rather than policy disagreement or democratic deliberation. This dramatic framework for understanding politics made compromise appear treasonous while positioning violence as potentially patriotic, creating conditions where future political violence became more rather than less likely.

The legend-making process also established expectations for political leadership that might prove impossible for future candidates to meet, as Trump's unique response to genuine mortal danger created standards of political courage that could not be manufactured or replicated through normal campaign activities. The bar for demonstrating authentic leadership had been raised to levels that required actual life-threatening circumstances, potentially making political service less attractive to qualified individuals who were unwilling to accept such extraordinary personal risks.

Lessons for American Democracy

The 2024 election offered both encouraging and troubling lessons about the resilience of American democratic institutions under extreme pressure. On the positive side, Trump's survival and electoral victory demonstrated that democratic processes could continue functioning even after attempted political assassinations, while the peaceful transfer of power following his election showed that constitutional mechanisms remained strong enough to contain political violence within democratic frameworks.

The election also revealed that American voters retained the capacity to be moved by authentic displays of character under pressure, suggesting that democratic politics had not become completely dominated by artificial manipulation or professional staging. Trump's survival narrative succeeded precisely because it was genuine rather than manufactured, providing hope that voters could still distinguish between authentic leadership and campaign theater when presented with clear evidence of both.

However, the election also demonstrated how quickly political violence could become normalized and even celebrated within American political culture, creating dangerous precedents for future democratic competition. The integration of survival narratives, divine protection claims, and martyrdom themes into mainstream political messaging suggested that American democracy was adapting to accommodate rather than resist the presence of political violence in electoral competition.

The Road Ahead

As Trump began his second presidency with the enhanced moral authority that came from surviving assassination attempts, the broader implications of his victory continued to unfold in American political culture. His success in converting victimization into victory would inspire imitators while creating expectations that future political leaders should demonstrate similar courage under fire. The religious interpretation that many Americans placed on his survival would influence how faith communities engaged with politics for generations, while the security measures necessitated by ongoing threats would permanently alter how democratic participation occurred.

The most pressing question facing American democracy was whether Trump's survival would serve as a wake-up call leading to meaningful reforms in political rhetoric and institutional protections, or whether political violence would continue escalating until it fundamentally altered the character of democratic governance. The answer would depend partly on Trump's own leadership as president—whether he would use his unique moral authority to heal national divisions or exploit his martyrdom narrative to justify increasingly authoritarian approaches to political opposition.

The events of July 13, 2024, lasting just eight seconds, had created political consequences that would reverberate through American history for decades to come. The bullet that missed Donald Trump by two inches had changed not just his personal destiny but the trajectory of American democracy itself, establishing new precedents for how political violence would be integrated into democratic competition while creating legends that would inspire and influence future generations of American political leaders.

Final Reflections

The story told in this book is ultimately about the power of authentic human drama to reshape political competition in the modern era, demonstrating that genuine displays of character under extreme circumstances could still triumph over professional campaign management and media manipulation. Trump's survival narrative succeeded because it was real rather than manufactured, providing voters with evidence of leadership qualities that could not be faked or purchased through advertising campaigns.

Yet this triumph of authenticity came at enormous costs to American democratic culture, as the celebration of political violence and the integration of divine authority into partisan competition created dangerous precedents that threatened the peaceful character of democratic deliberation. The eight seconds that changed American political history had created both inspiration and danger, legend and threat, democratic resilience and institutional vulnerability in ways that would influence American political life for generations.

The ultimate lesson of the 2024 election may be that in an age of artificial intelligence, social media manipulation, and professional political theater, American voters retained a deep hunger for authentic human experience that could still reshape electoral competition when genuine crisis revealed true character. Whether this hunger for authenticity would lead to healthier democratic culture or more dangerous political competition remained the crucial question facing American democracy in the years ahead.

Donald Trump had proven that eight seconds of genuine human drama could indeed change the course of American political history. The question that remained was whether American democracy would be strengthened or weakened by the precedents established through his remarkable journey from assassination target to political legend to President of the United States. The answer would shape not just Trump's presidency but the future of democratic governance in America for decades to come.

www.ingramcontent.com/pod-product-compliance
Lightning Source LLC
Chambersburg PA
CBHW062059270326
41931CB00013B/3147